EXPERIENCING MINISTRY SUPERVISION

EXPERIENCING MINISTRY SUPERVISION

A FIELD-BASED APPROACH

WILLIAM T. PYLE AND MARY ALICE SEALS, EDITORS

BROADMAN
& HOLMAN
PUBLISHERS

Nashville, Tennessee

4211-63
0-8054-1163-1

Dewey Decimal Classification: 268.62
Subject Heading:
Supervised Ministry Experience \ Seminary Students—
Vocational Guidance
Library of Congress Card Catalog Number: 94-6860

Unless otherwise noted, Scripture quotations are from the Holy Bible, *New International Version*, copyright © 1973, 1978, 1984 by International Bible Society. Scriptures marked KJV are from the *King James Version*, and those marked NASB are from the *New American Standard Bible* © The Lockman Foundation, 1960, 1962, 1963, 1968, 1971, 1972, 1973, 1975, 1977, used by permission.

Interior design by Leslie Joslin
Cover design by Steve Diggs & Friends

Library of Congress Cataloging-in-Publication Data
Experiencing ministry supervision / edited by William T. Pyle and Mary
Alice Seals.
         p.   cm.
Includes bibliographical references.
ISBN 0-8054-1163-1
1. Pastoral theology—Field work. 2. Pastoral theology—Study
and teaching—Supervision.   I. Pyle, William T., 1956– .   II. Seals,
Mary Alice, 1955– .
  BV4164.5.E97   1995
  253'.071'55—dc20   94-6860
                                                                   CIP

Dedicated to
William E. Neptune
In-Service Guidance Consultant,
Educator, pioneer, encourager, colleague, and friend

Contributors

Doris Borchert, associate professor of Christian education and director of supervised ministry experience for the School of Christian Education, The Southern Baptist Theological Seminary.

Ronald Hornecker, associate professor of ministry and director of doctoral ministry studies, Golden Gate Baptist Theological Seminary.

Walter C. Jackson, professor of ministry and seminary director of supervised ministry experience, Southern Baptist Theological Seminary.

Ray Kesner, director of vocational services and theological field education, Midwestern Baptist Theological Seminary

Gary Pearson, associate professor of ministry and director of supervised ministry, Golden Gate Baptist Theological Seminary.

William T. Pyle, assistant professor of supervised field ministry, Southeastern Baptist Theological Seminary.

Mary Alice Seals, assistant professor of church music and coordinator of supervised ministry experience in the School of Church Music, Southern Baptist Theological Seminary.

Paul Stevens, professor and director of field education, The Southwestern Baptist Theological Seminary.

Contents

Foreword

Theological field education is beginning to emerge from the alchemy stage. Just as there is no magic way to convert iron into gold, there is no magic way to convert an inexperienced student into a mature minister. As a new science emerged from alchemy experiments, a new field of study (field education) is emerging from previous practical theology courses and field training. Psychology is the study of the way a person behaves and field education is the study of ministers' (or would-be ministers') behavior in a religious system. Field education also tries to help ministers function appropriately in ministry.

Most of us enjoy seeing people do well at their craft. A mechanic adjusts an engine and it hums smoothly. A seamstress sews a few stitches that are almost invisible to the eye. A glassblower patiently heats and twists material into a complex shape. An orator writes majestic words and presents them with drama. A surgeon is able to repair damaged tissue with such preciseness that an organ functions perfectly again. If field education is a craft, it isn't amenable to admiration as are other crafts. Its influence is usually far more subtle than the physical crafts. A person needs inner subjectivism to discern what happens in field education. Often those influenced by field education are unaware of this influence and praise (or blame) someone else.

The writers of this volume have been helping field education emerge from alchemy. Now they are sharing their observations about the craft of field education. The writers are Southern Baptists. Many may not realize the great progress that Southern Baptist field education programs have made during the last two decades. Laboring under the disadvantage of having to work with programs so large that they are unmanageable, directors have applied principles of field-based learning in creative ways.

The writers of this book have been active in the Conference for Southern Baptist In-Service Guidance Directors and the Association for Theological Field Education. They have led field education training conferences. They have trained in the discipline of field education. They have gained insight needed to see how the craft of field education works. Now they are giving us a book from their training and experience.

Doran C. McCarty
Nashville

Preface

Experiencing Ministry Supervision is the result of an ongoing dialogue among the field education professors of the six Southern Baptist Convention seminaries. Each of us realized the need for a textbook specifically designed for ministerial students involved in field-based experiential learning. While the program at each school has distinctive features, all share a common understanding of theological field education.

Our understanding has been shaped by our affiliation with two primary organizations. The Association for Theological Field Education offers dialogue, training, and support in a broader ecumenical context. The In-Service Guidance Directors of the Southern Baptist Convention is a professional organization for professors providing experiential learning for ministerial students in Southern Baptist colleges, universities, and seminaries. We gratefully acknowledge our debt to colleagues in these organizations who have nurtured, challenged, and encouraged us.

Some authors have used examples from their experiences with students and field supervisors. When examples have been used, the names have been changed to protect the confidentiality of the persons, churches, and agencies involved.

Items defined in the glossary are printed in boldface type the first time they appear in each chapter.

We are grateful for the opportunity to collaborate on this project. It is our wish that students would experience meaningful growth as they participate in theological field education.

1

An Introduction to
Theological Field Education

Walter C. Jackson

A Brief History of Field Education
> Secular Field Education
> Early Field Education for Ministry
> The Case Study Method
> Clinical Pastoral Education
> The Development of Theological Field Education

A Philosophy of Theological Field Education
> Field Education Is Theological
> Field Education Uses Symbolic Representation
> Field Education Focuses on the Learner
> Field Education Is Personal and Experiential
> Field Education Is Contextual Learning
> Field Education Is Relational
> Field Education Is Ministry
> Field Education Supervisors Are Models
> Field Education Nurtures Student Autonomy
> Field Education Thrives amid Trust and Hope
> Field Education Is Integrative

Mission, Goals, and Strategies of Theological Field Education
> 1: Nurturing Personal Spirituality
> 2: Developing Relational Skills
> 3: Reflecting Theologically
> 4: Learning Through Relationships
> 5: Learning Through Ministry Events

Education for ministry is a vital task for Christians. The process of ministerial education has gone through major shifts and has received criticism from time to time. How does one go about training those among us called to be vocational ministers? Of the many questions voiced about ministerial education, the ones most frequently asked include:

- What should ministers be taught?

- How should ministers be taught?

- Where should ministers be taught?

- Who should be trained for ministry?

- When should ministers be taught?

Theological educators have seldom agreed, and never completely, about the answers to most of these questions. Yet, they do agree that ministers are better able to proclaim and sustain the ministry of the gospel with an education that anchors them faithfully to the biblical witness and informs them of the history of their faith. Ministers must also be thoroughly aware of their own times and be competent to translate their classroom learning into the practice of ministry.

Theological field education is a refinement of one of the oldest kinds of education. In its first forms, those who knew how to do things taught others to do them by demonstration and example. Students learned by observing the "master teacher" and by then "practicing" what was to be learned. The mature teacher looked on and provided on-the-job instruction in the context of the student's efforts to apply what had been learned. The earliest kinds of more academic learning strategies found the great teachers and artists gathering students who followed them. Students learned through dialogue with their masters and with others, often learning more from antagonists than fellow believers. Even here, learning occurred in the context of the performance of one's craft, art, or profession.

The discipline of theological field education has appeared in the twentieth century as an educational strategy to give attention to the practical side of ministry, that is, to the spirituality of the minister and to the arts and skills of ministry in action. The purpose of this chapter is to describe briefly the history of practical learning and to suggest a model for theological field education in terms of its history, philosophy, goals, and strategies.

A Brief History of Field Education

After dominating early learning, contextual education lost ground as universities developed. As new written resources were added to ancient literary treasures, the primary method of teaching and learning became classroom teaching, disciplined reading, literary research, and writing. Theoretical learning was soon believed to be superior to practical learning. As a result, classroom university methods became the primary way to educate persons in the great intellectual fields which dominated university education (philosophy, law, medicine, and theology).

Secular Field Education

Contextual learning did not disappear even though it was considered a less-esteemed way to an education. Field-based education developed side by side with university education, though it was largely isolated from the universities. Apprenticeships were developed to provide practical education and became the forerunners of trade guilds and modern technical schools. The combination of the best attributes of contextual and classroom learning into a single academic program of education was conspicuously absent.

A clear hierarchy of learning became established. The higher value was given to *cognitive,* or *theoretical learning,* which was largely Cartesian. It functioned as if learning is the acquisition of external knowledge which was to be divided (fragmented) into an ever enlarged group of distinct categories. A lower value was placed on *practical,* or *operational learning,* which dealt with one's ability to learn the arts and skills of a discipline while actually practicing a profession.

Through the years university education changed. Chemistry, physics, biology, anthropology, astronomy, and a host of other sciences were added to a standardized university curriculum. Social sciences were added later, such as psychology, sociology, and political science. The fields of engineering and business also earned a place in the university, but usually as separate schools.

Within the discipline of theology as studied in a university, the Scriptures and dogmatic theology were the predominant subdisciplines which took the major time and energy of scholars. Frederick Schleiermacher identified ministry vocations as worthy of theological study at the beginning of the nineteenth century. However, by the end of the century, Scripture, church history, and dogmatic theology remained at the center of the theological curriculum in the United States. Practical field learning, where present, was underemphasized.

Medical education was equally theoretical. Candidate physicians studied mostly in classrooms, laboratories, and libraries. Practical medical education was usually confined to student observation of professors with their patients. Practical application of classroom and laboratory learning came mostly after graduation in internships and residencies. In some places today, actual patient contact is delayed until quite late in the medical school curriculum.

One of the major reasons for the de-emphasis of practical education was the uneasiness of educators with performance-based learning and the integrated, practical intelligence[1] required for successfully acquiring and using it. The difficulty of measuring academic achievement in contextual education by standardized examinations also contributed to educators' uneasiness.

Early Field Education for Ministry

Among post-reformation Christian groups, theological education developed in ways similar in methodology to pre-reformation universities. The earliest theological training was provided by pastors in the non-established faith groups. They tutored candidate ministers in their own homes, using the Bible as the primary textbook and their own local churches as arenas for ministry practice. A few of these teaching pastors had university training and passed on some of the broad scholarly traditions to their students. However, the primary resources were the study of the Bible and the observation and imitation of the preaching and other pastoral skills of their

---

1. Robert J. Sternberg and Richard Wagner, eds., *Practical Intelligence: Nature and Origins of Competence in the Everyday World* (London: Cambridge University Press, 1986), 13–28.

mentors. The study of ministry by its practice provided ongoing motivation as well as learning content.

When evangelical Protestant denominations became able to produce their own colleges, universities, and seminaries, they quickly began to imitate the methods of theological education in the great universities. Cognitive learning and the development of intellectual skills came to dominate the learning activities of faculties and student bodies. For the most part, practical ministry did not achieve a base in the theological academy. Practical ministry skills were either perceived to be God-given gifts, and therefore unable to be learned, or were so easy to learn they were taken for granted.

Many students in evangelical seminaries served simultaneously as ministers. Mostly unaware of the value and high quality of learning provided them by their ministry service, they labored bi-vocationally as scholars and practitioners. When they attempted to bring questions from ministry in their churches into the classrooms, they were frequently met with excellent individualized mentoring, but received little formal instruction of a practical nature. These concerns were dismissed as being too practical to occupy space in the theological curriculum. Many agreed that some learning model was needed to address the educational-vocational needs of ministers, but this was not seen as germane to the central tasks of biblical, theological, historical, apologetical, or ethical studies.

The Case Study Method

New methods of education began to appear in some American places of higher learning. One of these was the **case study method** utilized by the law and business schools at Harvard University. The study of actual events as a source of learning had its early beginnings as a primary educational methodology in the late nineteenth century.

The case study method used actual historical events as a means of teaching decision-making processes and of assisting students in applying general principles to specific incidents. The case study method of learning, while widely suspect at first, began to influence others to imitate its success. Soon called "clinical" education, the case study method was adopted by other vocational disciplines whose theoretical data bases were foundational in the academy. The ancient disciplines of law and medicine, as well as the growing vocation of social work (operational sociology), embraced the case method as a primary learning tool. These disciplines were able to adapt the new teaching strategies with great success.

Clinical Pastoral Education

The mainline Protestant seminaries and divinity schools were slow to incorporate the new methods even though the Flexner Report of 1925 indicated the desperate need to prepare ministers to be responsive to the environment in which they would serve. Beginning in 1922, a small group of Protestant ministers outside the academy developed what we have come to know as the **Clinical Pastoral Education (CPE)** model. By 1925 the Council for Clinical Training and the Institute of Pastoral Care launched CPE as a new method of theological education. CPE was conducted almost exclusively in general and psychiatric hospital settings. Its ministry and learning focused on self-discovery, self-identity, and practicing the arts of responsive care for hospitalized patients suffering from illness, injury, abuse, and neglect. CPE had two major educational emphases. These primary emphases were:

- the growth and development of the candidate minister's personal and pastoral identity and function, and

- the minister's relationship with and to suffering patients in the presence of God.

CPE sought to nurture ministry styles which required the biblical and theological resources of the Christian faith to be active in relationships between ministers and parishioners. This was intended to enrich ministry by providing ministry candidates with a place to learn the art of caring for sufferers. By 1930, the two original CPE groups were established and receiving students from many denominations.[2]

Many educators in mainline seminaries dismissed CPE as non-classical and non-academic. CPE did not "fit" the generally recognized philosophies and methodologies of the academy-based theological curriculum. CPE was opposed by many evangelicals because

---

2. Edward Thornton, *Professional Education for Ministry: A History of Clinical Pastoral Education* (Nashville: Abingdon Press, 1970), 84.

of its widely advertised scientific bias, its preference for Freudian psychoanalytical theory, and the theological and social liberalism of its earliest educators. However, as CPE has continued to develop, its more mature forms at the end of the twentieth century reflect careful integration of its biblical and theological heritage.

The Development of Theological Field Education

In 1935 the American Association of Theological Schools (AATS) appointed its first committee of supervised training, but the 1936 standards document did not mention **field work** as required for the standard divinity degree curriculum. Faculty with interest in field work were disappointed. By the late 1940s, Lutherans and Southern Baptists had developed their own academically respectable CPE programs. Their work produced undeniably good academic results and developed their students' ministry skills. Pressures to place some kind of field-based learning in the curricula of seminaries and divinity schools continued to mount. However, it was not to be until Charles R. Feilding's 1966 essay, "Education for Ministry,"[3] that the AATS convinced the final hold-out seminary administrators of the necessity of including academically sound seminary-directed programs of field education in their degree requirements.

Professors of several disciplines with administrative expertise were enlisted to develop field work programs. This led to the development of a new professorial discipline and the eventual creation of the **Association for Theological Field Education (ATFE)**.[4]

Many colleges and seminaries had begun to require ministry under the supervision of an experienced minister as degree requirements as early as the mid-1950s. The work was directed by professors of a variety of disciplines. Repeating the history of other groups, the emphasis was first on "field work" before shifting the emphasis to "field education." In the churches, candidate ministers were placed in ministry positions and challenged to learn, but often

3. Charles R. Feilding, "Education for Ministry" (Dayton, Ohio: American Association of Theological Schools, 1966).
4. See Maureen Egan, "The History of the Association for Theological Field Education and Its Contribution to Theological Education in the United States," Ph.D. diss., St. Louis University, 1987.

progress was slow due to the limited availability of trained supervisors. However, results improved in time. Instructional staff and students alike grew together in the development of the field education discipline. Since its formal introduction, prayerful attention, vigorous development, and rigorous field testing has produced the professional discipline of theological field education. Today, theological field education is in a stage of early maturity. As the discipline continues to develop in theological colleges, seminaries, and institutions, reevaluation of theory and practice will occur.

A Philosophy of Theological Field Education

A philosophy of theological field education has been written and revised in each decade since 1945. The major changes observed in each revision reflect a discipline seeking to establish itself with permanent roots. The philosophy described here is stated as a simple list of priorities to be observed by theological field education participants—both students and supervisors.

Field Education Is Theological

The word "theological" in the title is not just window dressing. Students and educators, led by the Holy Spirit, are consciously working at the task of doing ministry. They analyze their actual ministry service in light of the teachings and patterns of ministry in Holy Scripture and the Spirit-led experiences of the Christian community. Ministry begins with the received text and the received tradition. The values derived from these rich sources are constantly applied in ministry service to individuals and congregations, as well as to cultural and international issues. The ministries are tested in a meditative reflection process to discover fresh meaning, new direction, and improved ways of doing the work of Christian ministry. Students and educators seek to discover the presence of God in their lives. They want to see God alive in their ministries as a catalyst for personal, spiritual, and theological growth.

Field Education Uses Symbolic Representation

The principal model of ministry is symbolic representation. A minister is a representative of God, a reminder of Jesus Christ, an instrument of the Holy Spirit, a representative of a specific group of Christians (church) who has commissioned the minister to serve, and a shepherd of the non-Christian.[5] The symbolic representational model provides the widest flexibility for ministerial identity development, while setting the outside boundaries firmly. The content of ministry, whatever form it takes, is ministry on behalf of God. Ministry is not a "lone ranger" process. Ministers are to be steadfastly linked to God, to their communities of faith, and to the people they serve in ministry. Ministry is done in the name of and on behalf of the God we worship: our Creator, Sustainer, and Redeemer.

Field Education Focuses on the Learner

The student is the center of the learning process. While other considerations are vital, and especially the actual ministry to the persons served, the guiding beacon for attention in the learning environment is the person of the student learner. The student in supervision is to be cared for as a unique person, a believing Christian, a committed minister, and a disciple of Jesus Christ, whose need to grow and develop in ministry is the principal object of the program. The educational staff discovers the student's learning style and uses it to help the student learn. The staff also discovers the student's relational patterns, personal goals for learning, and individual needs for models of ministry and ministry skills. These are addressed in appropriate ways so as to stimulate student autonomy and wholeness. While standard information and ministry strategies can be provided didactically, students should have the opportunity to question and discover the appropriateness of these strategies for their own ministries.

Field Education Is Personal and Experiential

Every experience of the student has learning potential. Students are to be encouraged and challenged to pay attention to all elements of their experiences, and to reflect upon them. Experiences may reveal a person's ideas, feelings, meanings, deep longings, and primary values in ways previously unknown. The student's own process of learning is as important a focus of learning as the actual content of each experience. Hopefully, the instructional staff will

5. Wayne E. Oates, *The Christian Pastor*, 3rd ed., rev. (Philadelphia: Westminster Press, 1986), 65–95.

be skilled in the art of seizing "teachable moments" and providing timely responses. Sometimes students resist learning and growth. Such resistance may be an indication that the student does not know how to ask for help, rather than an act of deliberate stubbornness. Learning is a continuous process that is always available to us.

Field Education Is Contextual Learning

Theological field education provides a context for learning which utilizes a circular process: experiencing ministry, reporting the **ministry event**, reflecting on issues raised by the event, articulating the insights gained from reflection on the event, and planning new approaches to ministry. The learning which occurs during the process of theological field education depends upon the student's willingness to interact with experience. Students are encouraged to address each ministry event as an opportunity to learn, as well as to bring ministry to the people and relationships they discover.

Field Education Is Relational

Personal relationships are a valuable resource for learning in ministry. Giving attention to students' personal patterns of relatedness to significant others in the past may be beneficial, but so will discovering the ways in which they relate to others in the here-and-now of ministry. The student's future ministry will benefit from learning about the ways the student relates to self, peers in training, parishioners, professors, supervisors, and to God. Measuring these relationships against Christian standards is an important activity. Conversation about the student's effectiveness in relationships, especially biblical and theological reflection about these relationships, will help the student learn and grow. In addition, the relationships developed with primary supervisors or theological educators are of immense importance. When these relationships proceed with honesty, integrity, openness, appropriate empathy, compassion, loyalty, and durability, a lifelong memory of that healthy relationship will provide a basis for healthy and memorable ministry relationship-building.

Field Education Is Ministry

Students in field education serve as ministers. One of the key ingredients in theological field education is the commitment of the senior minister(s) and the congregation to the ministry status of the student. The support of a "status role" helps the student develop a ministerial identity. Status roles include Minister of Youth, Minister of Visitation, Chaplain, Campus Minister, College Minister, Church Planter. This challenges the student to "be" a minister while "becoming" a minister. Learning for ministry is minimized if the student's work is treated as something less than authentic or full-fledged ministry.

Field Education Supervisors Are Models

Successful learning relies on supervisors who serve as models. Ministry education is provided in a context of active ministry under the supervisory guidance of an experienced minister. The capacities, commitments, and integrated skills of the supervisor are vital to the learning process. Ministry education at its best is personal, developmental, cumulative, empathic, reflective, and integrative. The outcome goal for a minister is to possess a growing and deepening personal faith, an appropriate level of ministry skill competence, and a beginning but proven ability to make wise and discerning judgments about the art of ministry. The minister should also possess sufficient maturity to act upon those judgments in the process of ministry, while using reflective methods to increase ministry learning and competence in the process. In all of this, the student will be self-consciously committed to participate in the ongoing, creative work of God in Jesus Christ.

The field supervisor should model these characteristics of competent ministry. Prerequisites of the supervisor include preparation in personal and professional self-awareness, and in the art and skills of reflecting on ministry. The competence to do problem-solving and the ability to nurture the same competence in students is also important. The supervisor's most important skills are the willingness and ability to nurture and challenge the student's personal progress toward deeper spirituality, and biblical and theological reflection on the reported ministry events.

Field Education Nurtures Student Autonomy

The autonomy of the student is nurtured in theological field education. The instructional staff begins by honoring their students' own backgrounds of faith and ministry education by enabling them to minister in ways congruent with who they are. When students function to the best of their abilities, however high or low that may be, they are exposed to the possibility of personal growth and development. They will be nurtured and challenged to test themselves as ministers—as ministers who are teachable, and as ministers who can convert the actual practice of ministry into learning. They will also be nurtured and challenged to discover their inabilities and weaknesses. If they can learn from their failures, they will be better prepared to deal with any less-than-hoped-for outcomes in their future ministries. By resisting the compulsion to mold students into preconceived ministerial identities, supervisors empower students to choose authentic styles of ministry.

Field Education Thrives amid Trust and Hope

Learning thrives in an atmosphere of trust and hope. In theological field education, optimal learning occurs more easily and rapidly in an atmosphere of trust and hope, and in the absence of excessive anxiety. The best learning environments are neither neglectful nor abusive. While it is impossible to eliminate human anxiety while performing a professional duty like ministry, it is possible to eliminate the artificially induced terror often associated with the demands of an overwhelming situation. Students are blessed and challenged when they are carefully interviewed for a position by the senior minister and/or lay leadership and then offered a ministry position. When students are aware that the leaders and educators favor their successful development as ministers, the threat of the situation is reduced without reducing the challenge to do well and to grow. Much of the work in theological field education is difficult, tedious, and sometimes frightening. When the environment is infused with appropriate levels of trust and hope, the stage is set for optimal outcomes. This does not remove the student's responsibility for performance, learning, and growth. A healthy educational or vocational environment is one in which error, negligence, and failure will be acknowledged, examined, and used as learning opportunities. Students need to know that growing competence, successful learning, and service will be appropriately rewarded.

Field Education Is Integrative

Students need an opportunity to piece together the disconnected fragments they have received from their earlier education. A student's data base of learning in all areas, formal and informal, is to be used in the practice of ministry. Field educators face the challenge of helping students access former learning, in order to use that learning in a new context. New learning happens best in the company of former learning. Transformation and change occur when we unite old learning and new, experiential challenges. The student's own commitment to values and assumptions about life and faith will be challenged in the theological field education context.

While ministers frequently experience transformation in the lives of others, the greatest transformation usually occurs in their own lives. Theological field education can be one of the most powerful contexts for learning that a minister in training will ever experience.

Mission, Goals, and Strategies of Theological Field Education

The mission, goals, and strategies of theological field education may be defined in relatively uncomplicated terms. The mission of theological field education is to function as a partner with other theological disciplines in the task of preparing ministers for service.

Theological field education has three overall goals:

- to encourage a maturing spirituality in each student;

- to help students integrate educational and experiential fragments into a holistic and comprehensive understanding of the Christian faith;

- to help students integrate spirituality with intellect in order to produce continued growth in ministry skill, theological learning, and overall competence in the practice of ministry.

These master goals are accomplished by the use of at least the following five strategies.

Strategy #1: Nurturing Personal Spirituality

The curriculum of field education is designed to nurture personal spirituality in the life of each student. Spirituality begins in earnest with the felt call to become a believing Christian. At the time of conscious belief, the person is born anew to the growing potential of a deeper relationship with God. At the time of conscious commitment to become a minister, the Christian enters a new dimension of spiritual potential. An important strategy of theological field education is to nurture this spirituality by calling forth a reflective testimony of these two important events and of other events of spiritual importance in the student's memory. An awareness of the value of reflecting on one's personal religious history (story) is frequently experienced for the first time in the context of theological field education.

Public and private processes of spirituality are to be encouraged through a variety of experiences. One of the more productive arenas for such spiritual sharing would be in the periods of worship shared by students and supervisors together. Beyond that, the students are to be nurtured to pursue personal and intimate spirituality. In the quiet development of a student's relationship with God, the powerful energy of the spiritual life may be renewed and strengthened. Deep self-understanding and potential self-transcendence are possible in relation to God in ways no other relationship can provide. Ministers constantly learn that the absence of deep personal spirituality correlates with an inability to experience relational depths with those to whom they minister. The opposite is also frequently discovered. Ministers who have consistently warm and intimate spiritual relationships to God will be better able to enter into deeper and more spiritual relationships with those to whom they minister.

A strong and growing spirituality is not an option for ministers. It is a necessity. Ministers must speak to God in prayer about persons, and they must speak to persons about God. Personal spirituality is often the source of spiritual joy, but it also enriches ministry skills, strategies, methods, and all ministry activities.

Where I teach, students in first year Formation for Christian Ministry classes are encouraged to pursue serious spiritual journeys while they are experiencing the intellectual challenges in the classroom. Second-year students are challenged to continue developing spirituality as they minister for two semesters in **concurrent placements.** Here they have the opportunity to test the strength of their relationships with God as resources to understand and minister to others. Third-year students in the professional exit class focus on personal spirituality as a life-support system for use in the wide-ranging experiences awaiting them in ministry.

Spirituality is a vital and indispensable part of the minister's life. Spirituality requires constant and energetic development. Theological field education provides an opportunity for students to cultivate intentionally their personal relationships with God.

Strategy #2: Developing Relational Skills

The second strategy of theological field education is to call forth, develop, and add to the student's repertoire of relational ministry skills. Some students are so naturally gifted and have developed such superior relational skills that they acquire additional skills with ease. Other students, however, are less gifted and must work to catch up in their relational and awareness skills. Many people think that students either have or do not have relational skills. The truth is otherwise. Students can enrich and deepen their awareness, empathic, and relational skills through experiential learning.

Textbooks suggesting ways to minister abound, but in the absence of relational ability, even skill oriented methods may fall flat. Students should learn the theories related to general pastoral conversations, evangelism, pastoral care, counseling, preaching, etc., and look for the opportunities to practice and develop these skills in ways that enrich their basic relational skills. In this strategy, theological field education seeks to nurture all students to discover, exercise, improve, and bless their own gifts and skills for ministry. At the same time, students are encouraged to discover and to work at the necessary ministry gifts and skills they do not now possess in optimal form. Counseling is often helpful, and referral resources are constantly developed by theological field education faculty to provide such support opportunities for their students.

Strategy #3: Reflecting Theologically

Theological reflection is an important task for all Christians, but it is indispensable for ministers. Theological field education examines personal, small and large group, institutional, and global dimensions of Christian life and ministry in the light of the biblical-theological witness and in the presence of a living community of believers. The third strategy is to nurture the art of theological reflection on experiences in general, and ministry experiences in particular. While the disciplines of the human sciences such as medicine, sociology, anthropology, and psychology are to be pursued with some energy, ministers must know and master the Scripture and tradition of their own faith communities in order to reflect readily and ably upon their ministry experiences.

Theological reflection is not an easily learned ability. It is best learned in the context of the entire theological curriculum and in connection with each content area studied. Then the theological field education experience becomes a place for students to exercise the theological reflective skills they have already learned.

Strategy #4: Learning through Relationships

Theological field education challenges students to see individuals and groups of people as "living documents" for learning and community. The give-and-take of personal relationships between student ministers, other Christians, and non-Christians, are rich sources of learning and growth available to those who are open and prepared to receive such learning. Seeing others as important sources for learning is a special way to respect them. If the theological field education context can challenge students to discover the ways other people find meaning and purpose for their lives, and to do so in the relational context of friendship, support, comfort, and the deeper levels of relationship,[6] it will have given its students a gift worth many treasures. An important way for students to continue such learning after finishing their formal education is to make relational covenants with other ministers for serious conversations about life and ministry. A minister may find well-balanced camaraderie in relationships with older persons, persons of similar age, and younger persons. These relationships keep us personally alive to living and ministering. They also help us ward off the fatigue and burnout that plague those who isolate their inner lives from others.

---

6. Oates, *The Christian Pastor*, 190ff.

Strategy #5: Learning through Ministry Events

The fifth strategy is to design learning experiences which enable ministers to integrate the experiential, intellectual, and functional aspects of ministry on the basis of their own actual ministry events. A whole and "together" self is seen as a worthy goal for persons in any vocation, and is even more so for a minister of the gospel. It is important that the minister is an integrated individual who can provide appropriate love and care for others and do the work of ministry. Theological field education provides the context for ministers to do ministry and to reflect on that ministry with supportive instructors and peers. Reflecting on ministry events encourages the student to assess personal resources for ministry, process personal anxieties that inhibit ministry, and call forth the deposits of a lifetime of learning experiences.

Conclusion

My desire is that this introduction to the history and process of theological field education will help you understand the program at your school. My hope for you in your supervised ministry experience is that having tasted the joy of a successful moment of integrated ministry, you will not be satisfied in the future with mediocre ministry. You will be propelled forward by your own desire, as well as the supportive nudging of God's Spirit, to be continually involved in such ministry activity. The process of continuous learning throughout a lifetime of ministry will be an option you are better prepared to accomplish. You will be more open to God's leadership into new and frequently uncharted arenas of ministry. The hope of your faculty and supervisor(s) is that your supervised ministry experience will introduce you to experiential learning and create a hunger for holistic ministry.

2

Choosing a Ministry Placement and Field Supervisor

Ronald Hornecker

"Supervised Ministry was one of the most beneficial aspects of theological education for me," Stephen said. Why was his field education experience so helpful? It was the result of three primary factors: his ministry setting, his **field supervisor,** and his attitude. As a part-time church staff member, Stephen had an opportunity to serve in a ministry position that was consistent with his vocational choice. His pastor, who served as field supervisor, took seriously the opportunity to help shape, mold, and prepare a future minister. In addition, Stephen approached this requirement as an opportunity for learning and growth. These combined factors contributed to his positive learning experience.

Qualities of a Good Ministry Placement

The nature of the ministry setting will greatly influence what you gain from **theological field education**. Many of you will be limited to the **placements** prescribed by the school. Others of you will be responsible for finding your own place of ministry. In most cases it will be necessary to have the ministry setting approved by the school or the field education director. Within the guidelines of your school's program, do all you can to make certain that the place of service will afford the greatest opportunities for learning and for ministry. There are several factors you should consider.

Harmonizes with Your Vocational Intent

The ministry placement should be consistent with your vocational intent. A person planning to be a pastor should have an opportunity to participate in pastoral tasks and responsibilities. One planning to work in church and community ministries should serve in a service center or a church that has such a ministry. A church musician should be involved in leading a choir, planning and leading worship, and other related activities. Whatever your ministry focus, seek a position of service that will enable you to experience firsthand some of the challenges, responsibilities, and rewards that grow out of that particular ministry.

While the placement as described above is the ideal, opportunities to have such a placement are not always available. Some denominations do not allow persons to serve as pastors until they complete their formal education. Because of church policies or specific circumstances, persons serving in staff roles may be unable to plan and lead in worship, to direct the education program, or to preach regularly. Those not ordained may be unable to baptize or serve Communion. Yet, even with these limitations, seek to find a ministry position that will provide as extensive an experience as possible. You may be unable to do everything you want, but you should have the opportunity to do many or most of the tasks you see as a part of your calling. Observation will provide some possibilities for exposure to those tasks that you cannot personally do.

Some of you will begin your field education experience uncertain of your vocational direction. You may begin to clarify your calling by taking a position or internship in the general field of your gifts, or in an area of ministry you find enjoyable. Through this involvement some have discovered gifts or abilities they did not know they had. For others, the internship simply confirmed what they believed about themselves, or enabled them to discover that they could best serve in some capacity other than vocational ministry.

> Myung questioned whether he wanted to serve in local church ministry. When he saw the notice about the chaplaincy internship at the local hospital, it sparked his interest. He interviewed with the chaplain and was accepted as one of the interns. Myung satisfied his field education requirement in this way. By serving as a chaplain, he learned to minister to persons and families in crisis. He also learned about himself. Upon graduation, he applied for a clinical pastoral education internship and continued his preparation for ministry as a chaplain.
>
> The outcome for Diane was different. She also was uncertain about her ministry focus. She really liked children, so she chose to work as a children's minister. She served well in that capacity. By the end of the year, she realized she was in school more because of family encouragement than because of divine direction. She decided to leave theological school and pursue another vocation. Those involved in her supervision provided support and affirmation for that decision. As a result, she left school without a sense of guilt or failure.

Opportunity to Develop Leadership

The opportunity to function as a leader is another important factor to consider in choosing a field placement. Regardless of where you serve in the future or the nature of your ministry, you will be expected to function as a leader. Field education is an opportunity to begin developing your leadership abilities.

Several qualities characterize a placement that will help you develop. You should have responsibility for at least one ministry or program. It may be the teacher training program, the church's outreach ministry, the children's or youth choir, or any number of other ministries. The point is, it is your responsibility. As such, it is significant and important to the church or institution's mission. You should have the responsibility for either making or recommending decisions for approval. You can lead in planning in your area of responsibility for the duration of your ministry in that setting. You should have the opportunity to help enlist, train, and motivate persons to be a part of that particular ministry. The time investment is great enough for you to feel the weight of responsibility and to learn what it is like to succeed or fail. Through your involvement and with the assistance of an effective supervisor, you will learn about your strengths and weaknesses as a leader.

Opportunity to Relate to Other People

A third important quality of a good ministry placement is the opportunity to relate to people. Most ministry happens in relationships. Most problems in ministry grow out of relational difficulties.

An ideal setting will call for maximum involvement with people. You need to learn about your pattern of relationships so you can discover things such as how you characteristically relate to those who are critical or fault-finding, or why you may feel intimidated by authority figures or wealthy persons. Learning about the ways in which you relate to others will be an indispensable component of your growth.

Learning to work in partnership with lay persons as volunteers is also an essential part of this relationship area. (See chap. 5 for more information on **Lay Committees**.) Seeing them as partners in ministry and recognizing the resources they have to offer is critical for the success of any minister.

It is difficult to overemphasize the importance of learning how to relate to all types of people. Relating to the unchurched, ministering to and sharing your faith with them, is as important as ministering to those in the church. In many ways, the ability to relate will be a key to your effectiveness in ministry.

Opportunity to Integrate Ministry and Learning

The opportunity to do ministry and to learn from the experience are also important components of an adequate field setting. From a field education standpoint, these two elements are vitally linked and dependent on each other.

The field setting should provide you with the opportunity to be fully involved in ministry. Directly related to this involvement should be the opportunity to learn about ministry and about yourself. In fact, the emphasis needs to be on learning, with ministry and reflection on ministry as the primary tools for learning. This is not meant to depreciate the importance of ministry in any way. Yet, the purpose of field education is to focus on learning.

Involvement in ministry should result in the development of your ministerial identity. What does it mean for you to be a minister? What kind of minister do you want to be? How is your ministerial identity different from your personal identity? The field education experience can assist you in answering these questions. You should also have an opportunity to learn the basic skills and competencies needed to function at a beginning level in your chosen vocation. (See chap. 9 for a listing of basic competencies for ministry.) Having the freedom to try ministries for the first time, to gain experience, and even to fail is important. The experience ought to affirm your gifts and make you conscious of growth needs. It should also create further awareness of affective or personhood issues that will affect your ministry both positively and negatively.

An action-reflection process will be the primary means of integrating ministry and learning. With the help of your field supervisor and others, you will reflect upon **ministry events** and actions. These persons will assist you in discovering the significance, meaning, and implications of those events and actions for yourself and for others.

Juan was a theological student serving in his first pastorate. He was far more accustomed to seeing himself as a student than as a minister. One day as he was meeting with his field supervisor, he remarked about the people in his ministry setting. "They call me 'Reverend,'" he said. Yet he did not feel like a "Reverend." That comment presented the opportunity for the supervisor to talk with Juan about how he perceived himself and how persons in the ministry setting perceived him. He was struggling with his ministerial identity. Throughout the year, similar conversations occurred, and Juan experienced the joys and frustrations of ministry. Through reflection with his supervisor, he learned about himself. He also gained insight into how to work with and minister to the people in his congregation and community. Ministry and learning were inseparable parts of his field education experience.

Opportunity to Observe

In those settings where students cannot perform all the functions of ministry, an opportunity to observe is important. If you are not in a role that naturally places you on the church council, on the board of elders or deacons, or in attendance at staff meetings, you should have an opportunity to observe such meetings. The same is true for weddings, funerals, and premarital counseling sessions. The purpose of observing is to provide as much firsthand exposure to the facets and details of ministry as possible. Some placements will not naturally provide this opportunity for observation because of their size or structure. In those cases, seek an occasion to observe in a neighboring setting. Most ministries are open to helping in this way.

In some situations groups of students can get together and assist one another. Some have practiced baptizing each other. They have planned and practiced a Communion service. They have visited a funeral home where the director showed them through the facility, discussed the mortuary's procedures, and answered their questions. Creativity is the only limiting factor in gaining exposure and observation facets of ministry that you cannot personally conduct.

The above factors should emphasize the importance of choosing your ministry placement wisely. Some suggestions on doing so appear in another section of this chapter entitled "Finding a Ministry Placement and Field Supervisor."

Two Types of Placements

As you consider the qualities needed in an ideal ministry placement, also consider the types of placement. There are two: concurrent and block. Each has its strengths and weaknesses.

Concurrent placement involves serving in ministry while engaged in academic studies. Functioning as a staff member, a student pastor, or a campus minister are examples. One strength of this type of placement is the possibility it presents for integrating theory and practice. You can test or implement what you hear in class almost immediately. Another strength is the number of persons involved with you to give feedback or to serve as resources. A significant weakness is that your energies are divided due to many competing demands. Sometimes the requirements of the classroom seem to compete with the expectations of ministry.

In a **block placement,** the student serves in a ministry without taking additional classes. A clinical pastoral education unit is an example. The student serves as a chaplain for ten weeks, ordinarily in a hospital setting, five days a week. This may also include some nights and weekends. Lutherans require their ministerial students to spend the third year in some local ministry as an intern, after which the students return to school for their final year of study. Some block placements occur at the conclusion of the classroom experience and just prior to graduation. The advantage of a block placement is the freedom from other educational demands. The experience is usually full-time, firsthand ministry. The supervisory skills and ministry competence of the supervisor will largely determine how beneficial the learning experience will be. A disadvantage of some block placements is the lack of a peer group for support and evaluation.

Both concurrent and block placements can be either part-or full-time staff positions. They can involve formal and informal internships, or even volunteer positions. Persons may receive a salary, a small stipend, tuition assistance, expenses, or no financial remuneration at all. A paid placement does add status to the position. However, try to base your decision about placement on the factors stated in this chapter, not just the finances. Discover your options, and choose what will best meet your learning needs.

Qualities of a Good Field Supervisor

The choice of a field supervisor is of even greater significance than the decision about ministry placement. An excellent setting with a poor supervisor could be of less learning value than a mediocre setting with an excellent supervisor. Nothing can substitute for the one-on-one time you will spend reflecting on ministry events. As you consider supervisors, seek someone who embodies the following qualities.

Model

The ideal supervisor is a model and mentor in ministry. Such persons relate how they do ministry. They share their concept and philosophy of ministry. They provide a positive demonstration of how they handle conflict, personality differences, and multiple demands on their time. They provide guidance about how to execute the basic functions of their vocation. It is important to choose your supervisor wisely. This person will likely reinforce, change, or alter your concept of ministry and your way of doing ministry.

> Henry had been involved in a campus ministry to college students. His experience with pastors had been unpleasant. In fact, he really did not respect most of the ministers he knew. He decided to further his education and chose to attend a theological school. While there, a church called him as their part-time minister of youth. The pastor initiated a supervisory structure. During the two years Henry served on staff, he wrote an annual covenant and participated in supervisory meetings and periodic evaluations. Henry and the pastor were very different in personality and style of ministry, yet Henry watched and observed the pastor. After graduation, a church called Henry as pastor. He went willingly and excitedly to that new role. His relationship with the pastor had provided him with both a model and mentor. It changed his understanding of God's purpose for his life. It also changed the way in which he led and functioned in his new setting.

Available

Being available also is an important criteria for an effective supervisor. Availability involves more than taking time to meet with you. Availability not only includes physical presence, but emotional and spiritual presence.

Good supervisors convey by attitude and example that supervision is an integral part of ministry. It is an investment in you and your ministry and a multiplication and expansion of the supervisor's ministry. Good supervisors will make a commitment to the supervisory relationship and will honor your commitment.

Availability also involves the opportunity for firsthand observation. Written reports of ministry experiences help the supervisor gain insight into how you function in particular ministry encounters. However, nothing takes the place of personal observation.

Body language, tone of voice, physical demeanor, attitude toward those in your ministry, and other such factors are all things that a supervisor will want to observe and discuss with you.

Ideally, the field supervisor will be available in the setting where you serve. In some situations, that may be impossible. For instance, a pastor of a church probably will not have a qualified supervisor in the congregation. When that is the case, a denominational person or a staff person in a neighboring church or institution may very well fulfill that role. Such an arrangement will require some creativity in order to provide direct observation. The supervisor may come to your setting and observe. You may be asked to conduct some activities in the supervisor's setting. You may even use a home video camera to record ministry events. You and your supervisor can view them as part of a supervisory session.

Skilled Supervisor

Not every person who can be a model and is available will make a good supervisor. Good supervision involves elements both of art and skill. The person needs some natural supervisory ability and some developed supervisory skills and tools.

Effective supervisors usually have been trained or have experienced formal supervision themselves. They have a clear understanding of what you need from them. Those who have been supervised will know how supervision helped them as a person and a minister.

Try to find a supervisor who knows how to ask questions which enhance reflection. It is sometimes easier and more comfortable to have a supervisor who gives answers, but you will not learn as much. The supervisor also needs the ability to confront you. Confrontation really is a means of caring and expressing concern. Some of the most significant growth you can experience as a person and as a minister can result from a caring supervisor who confronts you about issues you need to face or changes you need to make.

An effective supervisor also perceives issues that lie beneath the surface. This person has insight into the personal dynamics of ministry situations and knows how to help you to discover these. Some of those dynamics may relate to you—to your fears, your anxieties, your insecurities, and your ministerial identity. Some may relate to the internal needs of others. Effective supervisors have an understanding of both the ministry skills and personal issues involved. They can also help you to understand these same issues and to grow in your ability to handle them appropriately.

Experiential Theologian

The theological dynamics within ministry situations are an aspect of supervision that frequently do not receive deserved attention. All ministry is filled with theology. Most persons behave, make decisions, and manifest attitudes based on theological concepts, whether conscious or not. (See chap. 8 for more information on theological reflection.)

A significant role for the field supervisor is to help you to reflect theologically on your ministry experiences. This person needs to have a clear understanding of theology and the theological basis for actions in ministry. This includes the ability to perceive where and how God is at work in the supervisor's life and ministry, as well as the ability to help you do the same. Supervisors need to be experiential theologians, helping others to discern the theology at work in a particular incident.

For instance, assume you are struggling with several issues related to time management. You may experience the demands of family, of ministry, of school, and the need of time for yourself. You seem to have difficulty saying no, delegating to others, and taking a day off. You are not taking time for physical exercise. There are several possible causes for this predicament. First, this could relate to time management skills. Second, the problem could be an affective one. Insecurities, concern for what others think, and the need to please could all have a significant effect on how you use your time and set priorities. Third, this could be a theological issue. The primary difficulty could be one of stewardship—stewardship of life, of abilities, of family, and of self. Looking at this matter through a theological lens could change your entire perspective. An effective supervisor would help you to explore all possible areas and would not neglect the theological. In choosing a field supervisor, do not neglect the person's ability to help you examine your ministry experiences in theological terms.

Team Player

Most formal supervision for students happens in a system. In-service guidance programs, field education programs, doctor of ministry programs, social work programs, and clinical pastoral education programs all have structured requirements. Most have multiple persons assisting with supervision. In order for the system to work to your benefit, the field supervisor must be willing to function as a team player.

Training is a required part of most supervisory systems. A potential supervisor may have many years of ministry experience, have supervised staff, or supervised interns in another program. Yet, it is important that the supervisor participate in the required training. Definitions and expectations regarding supervision vary. The supervisor needs to be aware of the requirements and philosophy of your particular program so as to help you meet those expectations and requirements, and to help you maximize the learning potential of your experience. In addition, a supervisor who is unwilling to train is also likely to be unavailable.

Regular supervisory reports, supervisory meetings, and written evaluations are a part of most programs. It is important for the supervisor to complete those forms and evaluations and attend the meetings. All persons in the supervisory system need to be informed and to work together as a team to help you grow and benefit from the experience.

Open and Vulnerable

Most of the qualities listed above relate primarily to ministry and supervisory skills. Some are more attitudinal in nature. There are some personal qualities that an effective supervisor should possess. The supervisor's personal faith and deep commitment to Christian ministry are assumed. Additional qualities are the supervisor's ability to be open and vulnerable with you.

Effective supervisors demonstrate self-understanding, self-awareness, and self-acceptance. They know who they are as persons and as ministers. They are comfortable with themselves. As such, they can reveal their humanity. They can more readily identify with you as a person and a minister and share their faults, failings, and frailties as a fellow pilgrim.

Finding a Ministry Placement
and Field Supervisor

After this look at the qualities of an ideal ministry placement and an effective field supervisor, you may be asking, "How do I find these?" You have already discovered that neither the setting nor supervisor will have all of these qualities. It will be a matter of choosing what seems best for you. Listed below are four basic suggestions regarding how you can take the initiative to find what you need.

Ask! Talk to other persons who can provide perceptions and information. Colleagues, whether fellow students or ministers, can tell you about their experience in a particular setting or with a particular supervisor. Directors of field education or other supervisory programs can offer insights about settings and supervisors. They can suggest where to look. Many offices have directories or lists of approved supervisors and settings. Also, you probably have already heard positive and negative comments about some settings and some supervisors through the campus grapevine.

Interview! If you are considering a particular setting or supervisor, go and interview them. Take the initiative. Perhaps you will want to ask specific questions growing out of material in this chapter. Share in the interview what you believe you want or need from the experience. Discover what can be negotiated. Supervisors who view the training of future vocational ministers as an extension of their ministry will likely negotiate some responsibilities.

Plan! Do not leave choosing a ministry placement and a supervisor to the last minute. If serving in a ministry setting under supervision is a part of your educational requirement, you will know that the very first day you enroll. Use that knowledge to plan accordingly. List the competencies you need to develop. Begin to compile a list of potential places and the kinds of ministry you want to experience. Recognize that you have choices in this matter that will have potential long-term effects on your ministry.

Observe! Visit the ministry settings. Attend worship services in churches where you think you would like to serve. Experience first-hand a Christian social ministry center, if that is your interest. See how the potential supervisor relates to staff, to volunteers, and to strangers. Is this a ministry or location where you could make a contribution and learn? Questions can be both raised and answered by going to a setting and observing.

There are two additional matters regarding finding a ministry placement and field supervisor some will need to consider. They relate to gender and culture.

The two gender issues are: women ministry students and persons of the opposite sex serving as supervisors. Women students frequently are at some disadvantage in finding an adequate setting or supervisor. Attitudes toward women in ministry and views concerning appropriate roles vary with the setting and the supervisor. Some women will be unable to find settings where they can gain the experience they need to prepare for the role to which they feel called. Finding a woman minister who can function as a role model also may be difficult.

In some settings a person of the opposite sex will serve as the supervisor. That can provide additional dynamics for the supervisory relationship. The nature of those dynamics will depend on the persons involved, their backgrounds, and their personal beliefs and biases. Some males may resist the idea of being supervised by a woman. Some male supervisors may be uncomfortable or uncertain about how to relate to a female student in a supervisory relationship.

Cultural factors relate to ethnic as well as geographic differences. Some cultures will view the roles of the supervisor and the student intern differently than the ideal described in this chapter. Supervisors may function in a more authoritarian manner, thereby limiting a student's opportunity for ministry. There is also the matter of an ethnic student serving in an Anglo context or vice versa. Frequently, the style of ministry and expectations are different from the culture to which the student will return. Geographic and rural-urban differences can also significantly affect the learning experience.

> James came from a midwestern, rural, very traditional background. His field education placement was in the inner city of a major metropolitan area on the West Coast. He encountered people, lifestyles, and needs he had never before experienced. He had to deal not only with learning the basics of how to minister there and to those people, but also with culture shock and all the different emotions he felt.

There are no easy nor universal answers about how best to address these gender and cultural issues. If they apply to you, seek the counsel of someone who can help you to identify the difficulties you will encounter. Decide what options are available, and make intentional use of the four suggestions stated above.

Conclusion

This chapter began by recounting Stephen's perception of his field education experience. His attitude helped him have a positive experience. Attitude will also be important for you. You can have the very best of field settings with the very best field supervisor available. Yet, if you have a negative or apathetic attitude, you will miss much of the value. On the other hand, you can view your field education as an opportunity to integrate the theoretical with the functional. You can view it as an opportunity to enhance your ministry skills and abilities. You can view it as an opportunity to learn about yourself and to grow as a person.

Ministry under supervision can be a positive and growth-producing experience. I trust that it will be so for you.

3

Vocational Discernment

Ray Kesner

Robert Schnase speaks of Testing and Reclaiming Your Call to Ministry as something to do in the years after college and seminary.[1] Engaging in ministry under supervision *during* seminary offers a safer and more timely means for trying out your vocational commitment.

Testing one's call is a biblical, ecclesiastical, and pragmatic necessity. In Scripture, those who aspire to church leadership must have proven gifts such as hospitality, gentleness, and the ability to teach

---

1. Robert Schnase, *Testing and Reclaiming Your Call to Ministry* (Nashville: Abingdon Press, 1991), 72.

and maintain a good public image. Leaders need a certain psycho-social maturity: they must be "temperate, self-controlled, respectable . . . not given to drunkenness . . . not quarrelsome, not a lover of money" (1 Tim. 3:2–3). They must also be people of demonstrated Christian maturity, not recent converts.

Ecclesiology requires not only an individual sense of call but a call by some church as well. John Calvin speaks of an "outward and solemn call which has to do with the public order of the church" and a "secret call."[2] James R. Edwards writes about the two call elements: "The secret call is given to the heart of the believer . . . the corporate call . . . is testified to by the church and it ratifies the individual call. Both are complementary and necessary for genuine calling."[3] Secret call and ecclesiastical call are the terms Richard Niebuhr uses for these two aspects of vocation.[4]

To pursue a vocation for which you are not well-suited is to follow a destiny of frustration and failure. Several factors make this true. First, if you don't have suitable ministry gifts you will have a difficult time finding a place in which to serve. Second, after securing a position you will have a difficult time with the demands it places upon you. Third, people will quickly know if you are out of your place, and they may resist your leadership. If you are unable to provide needed leadership, other gifted people will move in to assert leadership.

Theological field education is designed to prevent this kind of trauma. It allows you to test your gifts by actual ministry experiences before assuming more weighty ministry responsibilities. Doing ministry under supervision helps you learn through experience what fits and what doesn't fit. Field education helps to validate or invalidate different aspects of vocational understanding. Encounters in the real world of Christian service permit an evaluation of the ecclesiastical call before assuming full-fledged ministry

---

2. John T. McNeill, ed., *Calvin: Institutes of the Christian Religion*, vol. 21, *The Library of Christian Classics* (Philadelphia: The Westminster Press, 1960), 1062–63.

3. James R. Edwards, "The Calling," *Christianity Today* 32 (5 February 1988), 61.

4. Richard Niebuhr, Daniel Day Williams, James M. Gustafson, *The Purpose of the Church and Its Ministry* (New York: Harper Brothers, 1956), 64.

responsibilities. Feedback from field, peer, and lay supervision is representative of the church's response to us as ministers.

> Sally thought her call was to work with children in inner-city minis-
> try. However, through actual inner-city ministry it became obvious
> to her, the church, and her supervisors that her ministry gifts were in
> other areas. John, a lifelong city dweller, discovered through field
> experience that he liked working in a rural setting.

One of the best things about "testing and claiming" your call through contextual education is the natural support system that is characteristic of theological field education. It is by design that supervisors and students develop deep, trusting relationships. These significant relationships provide a safe context for exploring and, when indicated, clarifying your call to ministry. The ministry context after seminary is much less secure, and the cost of call clarification may then be tragically expensive.

Clarifying Vocation Through a Vocational Management Plan

Field education not only offers an opportunity for testing ministerial identity and ministry role; it is also a time for planning what you will do with ministry in the future. A research group headed by John Biersdorf determined that ministers who plan their ministries are more likely to have fulfilling and productive experiences than those who allow their vocation to unfold along uncharted paths.[5] Constructing a **vocational management plan** is an effective means for implementing such an intentional ministry direction.

A vocational management plan is a design for future ministry. The plan brings together widely accepted institutional planning structures and applies them to purposeful career development. Some supervised ministry programs use the plan as a substitute for the **learning covenant** and for overall career management. It is sometimes used as a supplement to the covenant in other programs.

The concept of intentionality in ministry and the practice of following a vocational management plan is a proactive approach to guiding one's ministry along predictable paths to vocational matu-

---

5. John Biersdorf, *Creating an Intentional Ministry* (Nashville: Abingdon, 1976), 22–40.

rity. Many people think they are captives of future circumstances. Proactive people decide what their futures are to be like, then focus their efforts on making the future happen.[6] Proactive people are "winners." Reactive people are either "non-winners" or "losers." A winner sets goals and reaches them.

In my work with field education, I use a two-phase vocational management plan. In Phase I, students plan vocations for the academic year. This first part of the vocational management plan substitutes for the learning covenant and is similar to it. It is completed at the beginning of the course and projects plans for growth and learning throughout the field experience. Phase II begins near the end of supervised ministry and projects vocational plans over the entire life span. When a learning covenant is used, only Phase II is developed. It is prepared after the covenant is fully operational, near the end of the field education course.

A vocational management plan consists of two major planning structures: the **vocational management planning pool** and goals. The management pool contains the basic data upon which vocational goals are based. Your plan consists of narratives that delineate your call, your values, your personal and family needs, wants and dreams. It also contains two other statements: your mission statement, and your vision statement. In the goals section you project specific goals that are achievable and dated. These goals are supported by the specific activities you will use to achieve them. Like the goals, activities are specific and dated. Evaluations are planned and timed procedures you will use along the way to keep up with your progress toward goal acquisition.

Vocational Management: Planning Pool

At this point I will describe in some detail the five components of the management pool. Later, I'll discuss how to develop goals, and the activities and evaluations which support them.

Call Statement

The **call statement** tells why you are in the ministry, how you are gifted for ministry, and the ministry role toward which you see

---

6. Stephen R. Covey, *The Seven Habits of Highly Effective People* (New York: Simon & Schuster, 1989), 67–94.

yourself moving. You may find Richard Niebuhr's four calling components helpful as you write your call statement. The first of these is *the call to be a disciple*. This is the call expressed in 1 Corinthians 1:2 as the call "to be holy." M. Basil Pennington refers to this as God's "persistent call." Every other aspect of Christian vocation owes its origin and meaning to this persistent call. Pennington adds, "He wants to come into our lives, our hearts. He wants to be our intimate friend. [This is] the universal call to holiness . . . the fundamental call, the common call of all Christians. . . . [It] is to this that we are fundamentally called, to this intimacy with God, that embrace of love that generates life, that transforms us, renews in us Adam's lost likeness, that makes us one with God."[7] Everything else about your vocation rests upon this fundamental call to salvation, holiness, and intimate relationship with God. As you write your call statement and throughout your ministry, give close attention to this aspect of your call. Failure to do so will result in ministry that is inauthentic and anemic.

Growing out of this fundamental call is what Calvin and Niebuhr refer to as the *secret call*. Others refer to it as a private call. Fred McGehee terms it "God's grace call" to emphasize that receiving such a call is an expression of God's grace to us.[8] The secret call is that mystical aspect of calling in which we sense that God has set us apart for some particular ministry. The secret call emphasizes personal experience. Individual call experiences range from Damascus-road encounters to rational decisions that ministry just seems the right thing to do. Whatever your experience, you need to be able to articulate it clearly. This part of the vocational management plan provides the discipline to get you to do that.

Niebuhr's *providential call* recognizes the ways in which God has been working to get you ready for ministry since before God "formed you in the womb" (Jer. 1:5). This portion of the call statement tells how God has been preparing you for a ministry vocation through life events, interests, natural abilities, and grace gifts that

---

7. M. Basil Pennington, *Called, New Thinking on Christian Vocation* (New York: The Seabury Press, 1983), 4, 6–7.

8. From McGehee's Baptist Sunday School Board *Career-Assessment Manual* available at (615) 251–2772.

have been bestowed upon you. As you prepare this part of the call statement you are also likely to recall "muddles" that God has helped you to resolve. Resolving these has equipped you for ministries you would otherwise be ill-prepared to perform.[9] For example, recovering alcoholics, because of their own struggles with addictions, are able to help other alcoholics.

Information from **assessment instruments** used in field education or in other settings is particularly valuable for constructing this part of the call statement. Instruments such as the Strong Interest Inventory, Myers-Briggs Type Indicator, FIRO-B, Taylor-Johnson Temperament Analysis, Theological School Inventory, and California Psychological Inventory are among the most helpful instruments. (See appendix 1 for a description of these assessment instruments.)

The *ecclesiastical call* is God's call through other Christians. The most common example is an invitation to service in a specific ministry position. When you are called to a ministry role in a church, the congregation is essentially agreeing with your call and saying, "We believe God has gifted you and called you to minister among us."

Your ecclesiastical call confirms your secret call. Until a body of believers calls you to a specific ministry function, you cannot say with certainty that God has called you to some particular ministry role. This confirmation continues to be validated as you demonstrate over time that you can do the work of ministry. Those who fail to receive ecclesiastical confirmations must be willing to reevaluate their ministry direction.

Perhaps you have had little opportunity to receive an ecclesiastical call. This is common for those in the early stages of vocational maturity. There may be other ways in which your home church or other churches have confirmed your ministry gifts and your call to ministry even if you have never been called to a ministry position. No matter how limited they may be, it is important that you, now and in the future, pay close attention to those ways in which others are affirming, or denying, your call to ministry.

---

9. The concept of "resolved muddles" is from Fred McGehee's Baptist Sunday School Board *Career-Assessment Manual.*

Values Statement

Vocational integrity demands that what we are about in our ministries be congruent with the things to which we attach the highest value. To the extent that values and vocational demands are out of sync, to that degree our sense of integrity is called into question and self-worth is diminished. The **values statement** should help you clarify your values and plan your vocation so that it supports those values. The following list of values may help you decide which things are most valuable to you.

A List of Values

Material possessions	Public recognition
Pleasing someone	A sense of accomplishment
Personal freedom	Being a good person
Inner harmony	Friendship
Concern for family	Pleasing God
Intimacy with God	Competition
Being intelligent	Pursuit of wisdom
Excitement	Immediate gratification
Future gratification	A sense of beauty and order[10]

Whether you use this list or develop a values statement from scratch, when you prepare a vocation management plan you should write a values statement. The statement should list the ten to twelve values, in order of priority, that are most important to you.

Mission Statement

A **mission statement** is at the heart of intentional ministry. The statement identifies in concise terms the minister's mission in life. Once you understand your mission, every goal and, ideally, every action of your life should in some way support that mission.

With a well-executed mission statement you are empowered with an instrument against which every "decision concerning the most effective use of your time, talents, and your energies"[11] may

---

10. McGehee, *Career-Assessment Manual*, 9–10. My list is an amplification of his "Life Priority" list.

11. Covey, *Seven Habits*, 108–9.

be measured. Your mission statement, rather than the whims or opinions of others, becomes your basis for time management, planning, and daily experience.

The mission statement becomes "the basis for making major, life-directing decisions, the basis for making daily decisions in the midst of the circumstances and emotions that affect our lives. It empowers individuals with ... timeless strength in the midst of change."[12] One example of a mission statement is, "My mission in life is to keep straight with God, and others; be a lifelong learner; live by faith and communicate that faith to others; maintain integrity with myself and others; be selfish enough to manage my life well in order to have something worth giving away; be a servant to others to the extent of my resources under the direction and bondage of slavery to God."[13]

Vision Statement

The **vision statement** is similar to the mission statement. George Barna distinguishes between the two. A mission statement "is essentially a philosophic statement that undergirds the heart of your ministry." Vision, on the other hand, "is specific, detailed, customized, distinctive and unique. ... Mission statements are too vague. ... the vision statement is strategic in character."[14]

Preparing a vision statement is much more than a field education exercise. It is, rather, the product of your pilgrimage with God. Biblical models for this kind of pilgrimage are Jesus' forty days in the wilderness and Paul's three years in Arabia. Both engaged in significant solitary relationship with the Spirit of God, and from that relationship came an awareness of the precise nature of their future ministries—their vision for ministry.

Barna suggests a four-track process for discovering God's vision for our lives and ministries.

---

12. Covey, *Seven Habits*, 108.
13. Ray Kesner, *Theological Field Education Handbook* (Kansas City: Midwestern Baptist Theological Seminary, 1992), 26.
14. George Barna, *The Power of Vision* (Ventura, Calif.: Regal Books, 1992), 38–39.

- We must know ourselves; our abilities, gifts, limitations, values, and desires.

- We must know God intimately. Vision grows out of a deep and intimate walk with God over time.

- We must know our circumstances. The vocational management plan gets at this track through the discipline of defining our dreams, needs, and wants.

- We must receive "the discerning counsel of others."[15]

Barna defines vision for ministry as "a clear mental image of a preferable future imparted by God to His chosen servants" that is "based upon an accurate understanding of God, self, and circumstances." Understanding and following this vision enables you to "assert control over your environment, based on God's empowerment and direction, and make a better future."[16] Viewed so, vision is a natural and necessary part of an effective vocation management plan. Here is my own vision statement.

> I visualize my ministry continuing until the day of my death, no earlier than age 105. I will serve God and people through innovation, impact and caring. I will innovate by staying in close relationship with the God of the ages, the Bible, the church, contemporary living, and with my own soul. From this milieu I will develop viable approaches for making life work better. I will impact others through teaching, counseling and writing. Love will undergird all that I am and do as I keep up an active relationship with God, myself, my family, the community of faith, with friends and with the world. I will refuse to give away my destiny or vision to others.

Before leaving the vision statement, let me emphasize the importance of Barna's fourth step in determining your vision for ministry—obtaining the discerning counsel of others. The counsel of others is important at several stages. First, you need to talk with others about your ideas. Otherwise you run the risk of a fantasy rather than a realistic vision for ministry. Second, you must anticipate the support of others in carrying out your vision. Biersdorf's research group recognized the necessity of ministers engaging in

---

15. Barna, *The Power of Vision*, 152.
16. Ibid., 28.

successful negotiation with others in developing their ministry goals.[17] Your vision is doomed to failure without the involvement and support of others.

As you develop your vision statement, maintain a continuing dialogue with the people who make up your supervision team: field and group supervisors, support group members, and **lay committee** members. This will help you formulate a realistic vision statement. In the process, you will sharpen relational skills required for bringing others along who will share your vision and help you achieve its objectives.

Dreams-Needs-Wants Statement

Looking forthrightly at our needs and wants helps us keep in touch with the reality of the human situation. Without this reasoned look, we are at risk of engaging in denial about such things as housing, transportation, education, and retirement. Visionaries sometimes lose sight of these human necessities. Realistic vocation management recognizes both the vision, with its divine dimensions, and normal human needs or wants. Maintaining a balance between the two is crucial, difficult, and possible.

Your **dreams-needs-wants statement** might look something like this. Note that the woman who wrote this statement has a separate paragraph for each of the three categories.

I dream of being fully healed of my left-over emotional pains. I dream of having a happy family and of being happy with my family. I dream of a stable and challenging ministry position. I dream of helping my children grow up and of getting to see them dream. I dream of seeing some of my dreams come true.

I need a loving family, friends to support and care about me, enough to eat, clothes to wear, a safe place to live, a car to drive, a good job, and lots of strokes. I need to stay in close communion with God and the church.

I want most of my needs to be met. I want to be able to enjoy good food, some of the time cooked by someone else. I want nice clothes, a nice house, a nice car, a satisfying job, recognition for who I am and what I do, and lots and lots of strokes. I want to know how to

17. Biersdorf, *Creating*, 16–23.

deal with life's most difficult questions. I want to keep singing, "My best friend is Jesus." I also want to give myself away in service to God and others.[18]

Projecting our dreams, needs, and wants up front allows us to be more intentional about the things we decide to sacrifice on the altar of Christian service. God may indeed call us to sacrifice some of our wants and even curtail some of our needs. We will have a better attitude of service, however, when we have willfully offered them upon the cross Christ has called us to carry. More often such sacrifices are borne, not of willful and informed commitment, but of default. When we bear our sacrifices with informed commitment, God is able to help create in us an attitude of rejoicing in all circumstances. Default and circumstantial deprivation, on the other hand, may produce cynicism, bitterness, and a lingering spirit of defeat.

Vocational Management: Goals, Activities, and Evaluation

This section of your vocational management plan has three parts: (1) your goals, (2) some activities you will use to reach the goals, and (3) specific evaluation plans.

The vocational management planning pool provides the background information used in determining the goals you will attempt to achieve. The goals tell specifically what you will do to accomplish your vision for ministry. Every goal must pass the test of support for your mission in life or your vision for ministry. Goals must also be congruent with your call to ministry, your dreams, needs, and wants, and especially your values. Well-chosen goals make optimum use of the gifts, abilities, and interests referred to in your call statement. Avoid goals for which you possess limited gifts and which require you to engage in activities that are of little interest to you.

Pay particular attention when writing your goals for your mission and your vision for ministry statements. Refer to them regularly as you work to achieve your goals. I recommend converting both statements to some portable form so that you can carry them with you most of the time. Type them single-spaced, using small

---

18. Kesner, *Handbook*, 26–27.

print, and attach them to your daily planning calendar or in some other format. Keep them immediately accessible. The object is to have them close at hand and use them as a device for evaluating your investments of time and energy. These two statements will empower you if you prepare them well and refer to them often. Ideally, everything you do in some way supports your mission statement. Every activity that occupies your time and energy vocationally should in some way help you achieve your vision for ministry.

Jesus said, "let your 'Yes' be 'Yes,' and your 'No,' 'No' " (Matt. 5:37). This is a difficult assignment. It often seems easier to let others say our "Yes" and "No" for us. When we do, we give away personal power we could better invest in the vision God has for our ministries. A clear and constant awareness of our mission in life and vision for ministry empowers us to say our own "Yes" and "No." What's more, the very practice of determining our own "Yes" and "No" makes more power available for other things. One result may be that other people will notice in us what they observed in Jesus: "He taught as one who had authority" (Matt. 7:29).

The goals section for Phase I of the vocational management plan is developed in the same manner as the learning covenant. Phase I details learning and growth goals for the academic year. Goals for Phase I deal with five different learning areas: spiritual, cognitive, affective, skill, and applied theology.

- *Spiritual development goals* may include attention to the classic disciplines of prayer, fasting, meditation, reading or memorizing Scripture, journaling, or contracting with a spiritual guide.

- *Cognitive goals* seek to increase your knowledge of ministry, self, and theological application.

- *Affective goals* deal with the awareness and management of emotions you have when you conduct ministry.

- *Skill goals* have to do with your competency in performing ministry tasks.

- *Applied theology goals* relate to your ability to deal with life theologically. Classroom theology finds its application in ministry service. Contextual learning challenges you to test the theology you are learning in the classroom against the bumps and jolts of ministry experience.

Phase II of the vocational management plan projects ministry direction for the rest of your life. Planning should always be done, figuratively speaking, in pencil, since we can never fully anticipate the future. This part of the plan will require ongoing revision in order to adjust to life's unfolding circumstances. However, constantly revising your plan is much better than having no plan at all.

I suggest developing three kinds of goals: immediate, short-term and long-term.

- *Immediate goals* establish what you expect to accomplish within the next few weeks, months, or year.

- *Short-term goals* will be accomplished within the next few years, perhaps one to ten years. These usually cover such things as completing your education, securing a ministry position that fits reasonably well with your gifts and interests, and plans for continuing education.

- *Long-term goals* include such concerns as updating your education, your children's college education, paying off a home mortgage, or plans for retirement.

Activities and evaluations for this section may not be as detailed or complete as those developed for the academic year. The more complete you are able to make them, however, the more valuable your plan will be and the more it will enhance your effectiveness as an intentional minister.

As nearly as possible goals should be specific, achievable and dated. Activities are specific and dated actions you will take to reach the goals. Evaluation plans are definite and dated procedures you will follow to determine whether and to what extent you are achieving your goals. Plan evaluation events at various points along the way to allow necessary midcourse adjustments.

You should pay attention to certain predictable phases of career development as you construct this second aspect of your vocational plan. According to Bob Dale, ministers must negotiate four stages of vocational growth. Vocation maturity will normally move progressively through these four phases: getting started (possibly ages

15–25), developing vocational stability (possibly ages 25–35), developing your most significant ministry during the summit phase (possibly ages 35–55) and winding down during the simplification phase (possibly ages 55 and older).[19] Your vocation is likely to take you through these maturity levels whether you plan for them or not. Following a ministry plan will help you negotiate them and contribute to a more fulfilling and productive journey through the various phases of vocational development.

Supervisory Disciplines and Vocational Discernment

The vocational management plan is but one field education discipline that helps with vocational discernment. Even if you do not prepare a vocational management plan, the discipline of preparing call, mission, and vision for ministry statements will compel you to examine and clarify your particular ministry role. Supervisory relationships, contracting with a spiritual guide, journaling, and theological reflection also contribute to vocational discernment.

Relationships

Supervisory relationships often become mentoring relationships. The concept of mentoring comes from the ancient Greek poem, *The Odyssey*. The king's and queen's trusted friend, Mentor, became a substitute father to their son, Telemachus, while King Ulysses was away at war. Mentor's name is now synonymous with a wise person, trusted adviser, or teacher. Relating at this level allows the freedom to discuss a variety of vocational issues. Throughout the year, your supervisor will help you test your vocational perceptions against the strengths and weaknesses evident in your ministry reports. Dialogue with your supervisor is also important as you develop your call, mission, and vision statements.

A spiritual guide contract might also become a part of the supervisory relationship. You may contract with your supervisor or someone else. Include the terms of the contract in Phase I of your vocational management plan or in your learning covenant. In addi-

19. McGehee, *Career-Assessment Manual*, 36.

tion, you will probably want to enter into private agreements with your spiritual guide.

A spiritual guide meets with you regularly and listens to what is going on with you spiritually. He or she guides you in developing spiritual disciplines and helps you understand your deepest thoughts, feelings, and spiritual experiences. A spiritual guide contract is a submissive agreement outlining the novice's obligations and responsibilities in the relationship with the mentor. This agreement gives added weight to the guide's observations and suggestions. Where vocation is concerned, the guide may offer valuable observations about misperceived gifts, affirmations of gifts that are evident, and insights about nonevident gifts that emerge from the supervisory relationship. He or she may also lend powerful confirmation to accurately focused vocational plans, and with similar force call into question any plans that seem erroneously perceived.

When you enter into a contract for submission, you agree to take seriously opinions expressed by the spiritual guide. Such a contract gives significant, but not total, power to the guide. Ultimate power rests with you. A submission contract must, without fail, leave you with both the freedom and the responsibility to decide yes or no.

Journaling

Journaling is an especially helpful tool for vocational understanding. A **journal** allows you to report to supervisors your insights and responses to ministry events. You can report, in the thick of things, what you have done well and not so well. You can record experiences you have enjoyed and others which were distasteful.

Journals permit you also to be a supervisor to yourself. You are able to analyze and evaluate your own actions, feelings, and responses, based on journal entries. (See chap. 7.)

Theological Reflection

Theological reflection is also important to vocational discernment. Every vocational decision must meet the test of theological integrity. Theological reflection becomes a validation grid both for testing and forcefully supporting vocational direction. This theological grounding gives an ongoing sense of celebration to vocation. This is what people are talking about when they testify to the fulfillment that comes from living life within the will of God. In good times and bad, theological reflection allows the Christian minister truly to "rejoice in the Lord always" (Phil. 4:4). (See chap. 8).

Vocational discernment is a lifelong adventure. Field education offers unique opportunities for vocational understanding of the present and the future. Experiencing supervised ministry lets you assess your gifts, interests, and effectiveness, providing you with the information necessary for making vocational decisions.

4

Designing a
Learning Covenant

Gary Pearson

What Is a Learning Covenant?

Five Benefits of Covenanting

    Covenanting Allows You to Take Charge of Your Own
        Learning

    Covenanting Builds Trust Between You and Your Supervisor

    Covenanting Takes Seriously Your Uniqueness

    Covenanting Provides Structure to Get Something Done

    Covenanting Is a Tool for Good Stewardship

What Do You Need Before Writing a Covenant?

How Do You Design a Covenant?

    Agreement on Goals

    Learning/Serving Agreement

    Writing Goals

    Action Plans

    Setting Up Evaluation Standards

    Negotiation

    Writing the Covenant

    Approval and Commitment

"If you don't know where you're going, you may end up somewhere else!"[1] Where are you going with your life and with your ministry? The task of writing a covenant is a process of (1) deciding where you anticipate going intellectually, experientially, and ministerially for a defined period of your life; (2) developing **action plans** to move toward your destination; and (3) outlining steps you will take to insure that you get there. The **learning covenant** will let you know where "there" is so you can tell when you have gotten "there." Not only will it guide your getting there, it will help you understand what has happened to you and others during the journey. The process of covenanting is crucial to your experience in supervised ministry. If you don't know where you're going in your personal and professional pilgrimage, you will most likely end up somewhere else!

What Is a Learning Covenant?

Covenants and contracts have some common elements. However, there are significant differences. Contracts are based on responsibilities; covenants are based on relationships. Contracts define boundaries and bind; covenants provide for growth and becoming. Contracts are legalistic and enforceable; covenants focus on accountability and redemption. Our use of the term *covenant* is intentional. It has grown out of our covenantal relationship with God. God's covenant with us colors and shapes our understanding of our covenanting with each other. Your covenant will provide structure for your relationships: your relationship with God, your **field supervisor**, your **lay committee**, and your school's supervised ministry staff. Your covenant will clarify the expectations you have of one another. A dynamic covenant allows for and facilitates growth. A covenant should be mutually negotiated and accepted. If you keep faith with each other as you live out your agreements, it can lead to the integration of knowledge and experience. The making and keeping of covenants can lead to a deeper understanding of the meaning of being a child of God.

---

1. David Campbell, *If You Don't Know Where You're Going, You May End Up Somewhere Else!* (Niles, Ill.: Argus Communications, 1974).

Five Benefits of Covenanting

The learning covenant will be the most important document used in your supervised ministry experience. Of the numerous benefits to covenanting, let's examine just five.

Benefit #1: Covenanting Allows You to Take Charge of Your Own Learning

You have probably taken classes, read books, and engaged in learning activities, and wondered, "Why am I doing this?" You could see no benefit to you or your ministry from the time and effort you expended. Most of your educational experiences have consisted in doing what other people told you to do. "They" decided what you needed to know, when you needed to know it, and how you should learn it. Covenanting recognizes that you know yourself. By the time you reach this stage in the educational process, you have the ability to decide what you need to learn. The process allows you to select your own learning goals. You decide when and how you plan to learn. Greater self-determination of the learning process should result in greater learning. You will discover the seven benefits of self-determination:

- *Self-commitment:* you will be committed to make your goals become a reality because you have a major voice in setting your goals;

- *Self-motivation:* you will strive harder to reach your own goals;

- *Self-direction:* you can direct yourself in working toward fulfillment of your goals when you know the desired results and have developed a plan for reaching them;

- *Self-discipline:* you can use observations and feedback to make corrections;

- *Self-management:* you have more freedom to manage your time, energy, and other available resources;

- *Self-rewards:* you are not dependent on others to recognize meaningful results and increased competency;

- *Self-esteem:* you are building your own self-esteem throughout this process.[2]

Benefit #2: Covenanting Builds Trust Between You and Your Supervisor

As you define needs, identify resources, and negotiate how goals can be met, you and your supervisor can develop the emotional involvement needed to make something good happen. Richard Bollinger of the Menninger Clinic says the supervision process must have the effective investment of each party. Then, the parties will not go through supervision glibly nor terminate the relationship lightly.[3] The mutual investment of each party lessens the "over-under" aspect of supervision. By nature, the supervisory relationship involves a person with more experience, education, skill, and power. This situation can be intimidating. Covenanting helps build trust, lessens fear, and provides a basis for greater intimacy and acceptance. The supervisor and supervisee mutually work out how they will work together.

Benefit #3: Covenanting Takes Seriously Your Uniqueness

Covenanting protects your individuality. You are not forced into a mold by the ministry setting, or forced to be a clone of the supervisor. God had a reason for creating you the way you are. The covenant accepts that premise and customizes the agreements to further develop who you are and what your ministry can be. The covenant will provide structure for dealing with differences. Our differences usually lead to misunderstanding, judgmental attitudes, and serious problems. Or, we may choose to overlook the differences with an attitude of "live and let live." Either approach ignores our individuality and the richness of God's creativity. Covenanting recognizes differences and deals with them creatively by providing

---

2. Dale D. McConkey, *MBO for Non Profit Organizations* (New York: American Management Associations, 1975), 204.

3. Richard Bollinger, "What is Pastoral Supervision?" *Key Resources: Practical Theology and Reflection* (Association for Theological Field Education, 1974), 106.

structure for working together. The purpose is to build up and enrich, rather than enforce, inhibit, or ignore.

Benefit #4: Covenanting Provides Structure to Get Something Done

Covenanting helps you fit your experience in supervision into the life strategy you feel God has for you. If you are not sure what God's life strategy is (life strategy is not a life blueprint), covenanting can help you develop one. We are prone to resist making covenants or commitments because we think they will limit our options in the future. A well-written covenant will open doors rather than close them. It will use the skeletal information you have now to maximize the present and "flesh out" your future. For example, if you are unsure of your vocational direction, try out different areas of ministry. Covenant to work with a variety of age groups in a broad spectrum of ministries. Take primary responsibility to *do* something, to experience the ministries rather than just to observe them. Through *doing* you will experience how you, your makeup, abilities, gifts, and interests, fit into certain ministries. You may discover indicators of your future.

Benefit #5: Covenanting Is a Tool for Good Stewardship

We have already recognized your unique individuality. Your intellect, personality, social development, gifts, and abilities—even your energy levels—are different. One common ground that exists is time. Every person has the same number of hours in a day, week, or year. The use of time is the crucial factor not only to maximizing your educational experience, but also your ministry. You will have a great deal of freedom in determining how to spend your time as a vocational minister. Covenanting helps focus your time so you get the most important things done. If you are a good steward of your time, you can learn to be a good steward of all your resources.

One seminary says the covenant is the make-or-break component in supervision. It is the map to get you where you want to go. So, let's move to the next step in mapmaking or covenanting.

What Do You Need
Before Writing a Covenant?

Precovenant work is the work of gathering information that you will need in mapmaking/covenant making. Columbus knew where he was starting from, and had an idea where he wanted to go. He did not know that the Americas were between him and his destination. What could he have done with modern satellite information? It would have verified the earth's roundness, given him the topography, and even pictured weather systems!

You may be unsure where you're going. Perhaps you have never looked at where you are. Precovenant work could be the most difficult step in the process, for it requires an in-depth look at what you know, what you can do, and even who you are. It requires brutal honesty. Self-assessment can be painful. It can also be affirming and can give indicators to your future. So, grab a new legal pad and let's start filling up the pages with information.

Finding out where you are starting from is an act of maturity and wisdom. Don't assume anything. This is the time to ask God to give you courage to look at your self and the insight to understand what you see. You are going to take an inventory of every component of the supervisory system, beginning with yourself.

A good way to take an inventory is to begin with **assessment instruments**. You have probably already taken a variety of "tests" or instruments through your college or seminary work. Many schools use the Myers-Briggs Type Indicator, the California Psychological Profile, the Theological School Inventory, or Tennessee Self Concept. You may have taken the Taylor-Johnson Temperament Analysis, DISC, 16-PF, FIRO-B, or Profiles in Ministry (see appendix 1 for a brief description of these assessment instruments). What did each inventory say about you? Write down the results on your legal pad. You may agree or disagree with the information but write down a complete listing of what your test results indicated.

Then, make more lists—lots of lists. List your talents, your skills, your likes and dislikes, your experiences in church-related and non-church-related positions.

- What are you comfortable doing?

- What makes you uncomfortable?

- What do you avoid or try to ignore about yourself?

- What relational abilities do you have?

- Which abilities do you wish you had?

- What are your relational needs?

- What do people say about you?

- What are your strengths that others affirm?

- What weaknesses do others recognize?

- What do your critics say about you? (Critics are not always wrong just because they are your critics.)

Other self-assessment areas to jot down are your academic interests, your motivations, what gets you excited, and what energizes you. What do you enjoy knowing, reading about, studying, or experiencing? I know a student who came to seminary disliking school work. He loved to surf and teach others to surf. He was great in building one-on-one and small group relationships. He loved hiking and liked to study nature. As he assessed this and other information, he worked out covenant goals to develop a young adult ministry that would use his interests in a coastal community.

Do a **strengths inventory** on yourself. Make four columns on a legal pad. In the first column list all of your accomplishments, no matter how big or small, and no matter how long ago they happened. In the second column list the strengths, talents, and abilities that you used in doing what you did—even nebulous things like "cared for the person" or "patience." In the third column, list the strengths that you have developed and use easily. In the fourth column list those that show potential, that could be developed. Then, do some analysis. What patterns are present in your accomplishments? What strengths show up most often? Which ones do not show up that you think you need in your ministry? Does the information on your strengths inventory give any indication of how God has prepared you for certain ministries?

Steve Clapp's *Ministerial Competency Report* is a study based on twelve competencies most often mentioned by lay persons and clergy. This report identifies what they said would be required for one to be "fit, adequate, sufficient, capable, qualified, or able . . .

basic qualifications . . . ability" to begin ministry.[4] You might use this study or a competency list provided by your school to assess your beginning competencies for ministry. The "Issues in Evaluation" section at the end of chapter 9 may provide a basis for developing your own list of beginning competencies in ministry.

It is very important to take an honest look at what you're willing to do to develop your ministerial competencies. How much are you going to give to the experience? What excites you about learning through experience? Be honest about the time you will be able to give to supervised ministry in light of other responsibilities. I would not do a year of supervision while taking Greek or Hebrew because I have difficulty with languages. What about your health, energy, etc?

Finally, how do you usually sabotage yourself? What are the things that keep you from doing what needs to be done? What has blocked you in the past? What will be different this time? The experience of self-assessment may be the most comprehensive look you have ever taken of yourself. It is worth the time and the emotional effort.

You will need to assess each component (field supervisor, ministry setting, lay committee, etc.) of your supervisory system. For example, make lists of what your ministry setting has to offer. What is going on in the lives of the people it serves? What are its goals? What are its ministries or specialties? What is it known for? What about its racial, ethnic, socio-economic, demographic makeup? What is its history? What trends are developing? Look at the community served by the church or agency and ask the same questions. What experiences can you anticipate having at this place, and to what new things will you be exposed? Will it be a "teaching" church? What are the attitudes of the people toward student ministers? How does this ministry setting fit into what God is calling you to do in ministry? You are listing resources that you will want to access when writing your goals.

Make a written assessment of your field supervisor. What does your supervisor know that you want to learn or need to learn? How do you feel about opening up to your supervisor? Can you be vul-

---

4. Steve Clapp, *Ministerial Competency Report* (Sidell, Ill.: 4 Resources, 1982), 3.

nerable, expose your failures, or your innermost thoughts to the supervisor? How does this person seem to relate to "learners?" What kind of supervisory relationship would you prefer? What are the benefits you can expect from this supervisory relationship? Ask the same questions of each person in your supervisory system, making lists for each individual with whom you will work or to whom you will be responsible.

Finally, you will begin to distill the information you have gathered. You could use your legal pad to sort through information. On a new sheet list your needs—all of them—great or small. Mark the ones that are the most important with an X. Put a check mark by those that you want to work on. Prioritize the ones you marked. You are beginning to select the general direction you want and need to go during your experience in supervision. Take several sheets of paper. Put one need at the top of each sheet. Jot down ideas that could help you meet that need, keeping in mind the resources you listed for the ministry setting and your field supervisor.

Next, you will divide the sheets into three piles: cognitive, skill, and personhood. The cognitive pile will deal with data or information you will need to learn. For example, you may need to develop skills in working with senior adults. In order to do this effectively, you will need to acquire knowledge of the developmental needs of senior adults. The second stack will be ones that deal with skills you need to learn. You may need to learn to direct music, plan weddings, or to baptize. These are "how to do it" items. The third stack will be personhood items. These are areas that relate to who you are and how you need to change or grow, including items like becoming more willing to make hospital visits, being more accepting of poor people, or using your time more effectively.

Let's use another illustration. You may feel called to pastor a church, and recognize you need to develop your evangelistic ability. You may need to learn how persons experience faith at different stages of life. That need sheet would go in the cognitive stack. If you need training in the "how to" of doing one-on-one sharing of your faith, that need sheet would go in the skills stack. You could need to change your attitude about personal evangelism, or perhaps you need to overcome your fear of witnessing face-to-face. That sheet would go in the personhood stack.

You will draw from this information as you take the next steps of working with your field supervisor to write your covenant, a covenant that will be shaped by who you are and what you choose to learn. You are taking proactive steps, taking responsibility for your life and for your learning as you go through the process.

How Do You Design a Covenant?

Now the map can be drawn, starting with the beginning point (where you are now), and leading to the destination (where you want to go). The covenant will be the map you use for a specified period of time to get you where you want to go.

Your school may have specific ways to help you write your covenant. Some have a workshop where you and your field supervisor come together to draw up your covenant. Other schools train you in one setting and your field supervisor in another. In either case, *you* are responsible for taking the initiative. It is *your* covenant. Both you and your field supervisor work on it, negotiate it, and agree to it. You do it together so that both of you understand where you are going, why you're going there, and your individual responsibilities in getting you there. The covenant is a document of mutual obligations and commitments requiring mutual trust and cooperation. Therefore, it is mutually worked out. But you are primarily responsible.

Agreement on Goals

Taking the first step on the journey involves a mutual decision as to where you are going. Bring a rough draft of several possible goals that you have written in your precovenant work. Your field supervisor will have done some precovenant work in assessing his or her abilities, time, motivation, etc. Together, look at the resources in the ministry setting, the community, and the school. Begin defining where you want to be at the end of the supervisory program. Negotiate with each other and decide on which needs can be met—your needs and the ministry setting needs. Agreements on need statements and where you want to be at the end of the program are the material used later in goal setting.

Learning/Serving Agreement

This is the step of agreeing on the work you are going to be doing. In some schools this step is covered by the supervisory agreement or placement contract. Your field supervisor may have a job description that you can use in working out a **learning/serving agreement** that will become a part of your covenant. A learning, serving agreement includes information contained in a job description such as: the work to be done, lines of supervision, hours, time off, financial arrangements, and when you will meet for supervision. A learning/serving agreement is worked out together. It recognizes you are in the setting both to learn and serve. It helps define your responsibilities in the light of this. You need to discuss items such as church membership, expectations of related parties, and how to access resources. Try to clarify as many items as possible and put them into a written agreement. You will be moving from the common practice of assuming you both know what is needed (tacit agreement) to discussing intentionally each item. Talking and negotiating will lead to informal verbal agreements. Both tacit and informal agreements are difficult to remember or live up to. Accountability can be a problem. Once you have agreed on specific items, write them down with both of you working out how the agreements are worded. When the items are written out in mutually agreed-upon wording, you have a formal agreement, developed by a shared, conscious process. Both the ministry needs and your learning needs are recognized and defined.

One more word about learning/serving agreements. Be sure to include a safety valve. We expect things to go well, for problems to be small, and for relationships to be strengthened. Still, part of the agreement needs to spell out what you and your field supervisor are to do if things do not go as expected. How will each of you handle personality differences, feelings of mistrust, fear, anger, or hurt? You want to provide this part of the structure so personal differences do not lead to larger problems and disrupt the supervisory experience or ministry setting. There are several reasons to deal with these issues now and to formalize how you will work through problems. First, your feeling level is much lower and your sight much clearer. Later, tension may blur your vision and confuse your options. Second, if both of you explore options and agree on ways of handling disagreements, both of you are protected. There should not be surprises when (not if) a problem comes up. Third, providing for ways to address differences recognizes your individuality. The realistic acceptance of differences and the intentional processing of the accompanying feelings lead to wholeness.

Writing Goals

This step formalizes what you need or want to learn and how you plan to learn it. You begin writing goals with the end in mind. What learning outcomes do you want to achieve? Write down the need and the observable behaviors that will indicate that you have been able to reach your goal. What will you be like, look like, act like if you reach your goal? You want something good to happen. What do you want to occur? Most of your goals are probably abstract, and contain words like "develop" and "become more." Abstract goals are like mirages. They move, they change, you never get to them. Your present task is to "define the indefinable, to tangibilitate the intangible."[5] So, figure out concrete actions that you can document, that would result from your "developing" or "becoming." Write and rewrite, each time becoming more specific and concrete. Perhaps you will write more than one goal for a need statement. Once you have an observable behavior, or set of behaviors in mind, test to be sure the behaviors are true indicators that the need was met. Then, you are ready to write a SMART goal.

S — Specific (an observable behavior if possible)
M — Measurable (how many, how long)
A — Attainable (with the resources available such as time, money, etc.)
R — Relevant (to your vocational goal or personal growth, etc.)
T — Trackable (by what dates)

A goal statement should answer three questions:

---

5. Robert F. Mager, *Goal Analysis* (Belmont, Calif.: Fearon Publishers, 1972), 10.

- What?—the end result you expect;

- When?—the target date for completion;

- Who?—the person responsible for doing what is to be done.

You may be the person responsible, but your goal may also include to whom you will be accountable for the actions.

Goal statements need to be "simple, precise and memorable so as to keep your attention on them throughout supervision."[6] One student tended to talk when he felt confusion, tension, or pressure. He would try to dazzle perceived opponents with verbal footwork. His goal simply and memorably stated was "when in doubt I will listen!"

What kind of goals should you write? Goals that will meet your needs in three areas: cognitive, skills, and personhood. For this reason there are three types of goals. Let's illustrate by using the earlier illustration about developing evangelistic ability.

- *Cognitive goal:* A cognitive goal focuses on information you need to "know." Example: "By November 1 I will have read James Fowler's *Stages of Faith* and discussed with my supervisor its implication for evangelism."

- *Skills goal:* The skills goal is a professional goal that establishes "how to" objectives. Example: "I will have studied at least four methods of personal witnessing by November 1 and developed and implemented my own approach by November 15. I will discuss the outcomes with my field supervisor on December 15."

- *Personhood goal:* These goals involve "who you are" as a person. Your school may refer to them as psychological goals or therapeutic goals. Whatever they are called, they specify what and how you will change. Example: "I will take at least three new actions to overcome my fear of sharing my faith one-to-one by November 1. I will keep a log of the experiences and my feelings, and will share them with my field supervisor each month."

6. David A. Steere, *The Supervision of Pastoral Care* (Louisville: Westminster/ John Knox Press, 1989), 71.

Supervision programs vary in the number of covenant goals required. Your school will give specific requirements on how many are needed and how they are to be written. Here are three suggestions:

- Include both skill and personhood goals;

- Make sure your goals stretch you;

- Include at least one that involves spiritual growth.

Action Plans

Action plans are statements of how you plan to reach your goals. If the goals are your destinations on a map, the action plans are the routes you plan to use to get to your destination. Write out steps you can take to reach your goals. Decide if there is an order that you need to follow. For example, do you need to observe someone doing a task such as performing a funeral before you plan one? Do you need to discuss your plan with your field supervisor before you conduct one? Put the actions into a logical sequence. Then write them, answering the same what, when, and who questions you answered in writing goals.

Setting Up Evaluation Standards

This step is almost complete if you wrote your goals with the end in mind. Evaluation standards specify the observable behavior you're expecting and the date you should be able to observe it. You have set the "what" and "when" of your evaluation. All that is left is the "how much" and the "by whom." How much of the observable behavior can you legitimately expect by the specified date? How many times can you expect the actions to be repeated in order to consider them a successful completion of the goal? If my need is to become more comfortable making hospital visits, observable behaviors could be to enter the hospital room without stalling, and by smiling and speaking clearly. I would want to do that every time—100 percent. But, when I take into account why I'm uncomfortable and where I'm starting from, then 50 percent of the time may be an overwhelming success and three out of ten times (30 percent) may be acceptable to both me and my supervisor.

The "by whom" will be the person or persons that you designate to hold you accountable to complete the goal. Who will be objective? Which person in your supervisory system would best relate to each goal? Normally, the field supervisor will be the person to whom you are accountable, but it could be your lay committee or spiritual mentor. Also, consider how the person will know you have reached your goal. Will they observe and draw their own conclusions or will you report to them? If you report, will it be verbally or in writing? How will you report? Finally, you should be able to demonstrate to this person not only that something happened, but also your understanding of what happened. Evaluation is both result-oriented (what happened?) and learning-oriented (why did it happen?).

Negotiation

Once you have written your goals, action plans, and methods of evaluation, negotiate with the persons you need to help you reach your goals. They need to understand what you expect them to do, and why. You need to reach mutual agreement and commitment to the tasks. Next, check your goals with your field supervisor for compatibility. Your goals need to be compatible vertically and horizontally.[7]

Vertical compatibility means your goals do not conflict with those of your ministry **placement** or field supervisor. They all fit together. Meeting goals of one of the components helps the other components meet their goals. They do not conflict, inhibit, or damage one another. For example, you may write a goal to build a youth group. Your congregation may have targeted senior citizens this year, using all of the possible resources to reach them. The demographics of the community indicate there are few 12–19 year olds and 63 percent of the population is over age 50. Your goal, the church's goal, and the context would not be vertically compatible.

Horizontal compatibility insures you have the support from the setting and persons that you need. It means the finances, time, and space needed for your project do not conflict with the needs of others. The example in the paragraph above would not be horizon-

---

7. McConkey, *MBO*, 58–59.

tally compatible, since the church will be using all possible resources to reach older adults. Conflicts and problems are negotiated at this point and necessary changes are made in the goals.

Finally, check the goals to make sure they meet the guidelines set by your program of supervision. You could have a goal that attempts to meet a definite need in your ministry development but it does not fit your program's guidelines. Negotiate with the appropriate people. The program I work with does not permit spouses to serve in supervisory roles. One of my students set a goal relating to his marriage and wanted to make himself accountable to his wife. We discussed why this goal was important and why he felt his wife was crucial to the process. We agreed to make an exception in order for him to be accountable to both his wife and field supervisor.

Writing the Covenant

This step puts everything together. You are getting ready to print your map. You and your field supervisor review the goals and the learning/serving agreement. Do they coordinate with each other? Have you agreed to goals that necessitate changes in the learning/serving agreement? Discuss and include information on when and where the covenant can be changed. You cannot anticipate all that will happen while you are in the program. Then, combine the learning/serving agreement and goals in the format your program requires.

Approval and Commitment

Usually, your program director reads your covenant and takes one of three actions. One, the director may approve the covenant. Two, the director may approve part of the covenant but may require rewriting or revising parts of it. Three, the covenant may not be accepted. If it is rejected, you need to know why. As part of being responsible for your own learning, you may want to negotiate with your director to reach a mutually satisfying outcome.

Once your covenant is approved by all the necessary parties, you and your field supervisor commit yourselves to implementing the agreements. You set out on the journey together. You begin to do what you said you would do. As you act, you will reflect with each other about what is happening: detours, unexpected difficulties, serendipity joys, and new insights. Forming a covenant and carrying it out in a covenantal relationship makes this kind of supervision unique. It is ministry to all the parties involved.

George Barna critiques ministry training in his recent book *Today's Pastors*. He quotes a minister saying he wasted thousands of dollars learning stuff he did not use. Another said his seminary training was "3 lost years."[8] Covenanting is one way to insure you are not wasting your time or money. Through this process you decide what you need to know and how you're going to learn it. It puts you into the real world to do ministry with real people. It is a tool, a map that can lead you to some of your richest learning experiences. Use it! Then you will know where you are going and what it takes to get there. Covenanting will be a valuable tool now and throughout your ministry.

---

8. George Barna, *Today's Pastors* (Ventura, Calif.: Regal Books, 1993), 141.

5

Lay Committees

Doris Borchert

You have been reading about various aspects of the theological field education program. The **lay committee** is another exciting component of supervised ministry that can add a new dimension to your experience. You may receive supervision in your supervised ministry experience in a variety of ways. In most programs supervision is provided by a **field supervisor**. Other programs utilize lay committees for supervision, and some utilize a combination of a lay committee and field supervisor.

What Is a Lay Committee?

The lay committee is usually a group of five to seven persons who together have agreed to be a significant part of your supervisory team. They are commissioned to give you feedback concerning your ministry, to offer you insights about your particular placement, to support you, to reflect with you, to pray with you, to covenant with you, and to evaluate your work.

Allow me to share with you some examples of the ways in which lay committees have affected the ministry of my own students. You will read about the committee experiences of Kevin, Allyson, and Ted, and learn about some of the significant ways in which their committees functioned.

Kevin's Committee

Before meeting with his lay committee, Kevin had decided that the only thing he could do was leave seminary and give up his dream of being a minister in a local church. No one seemed to respond to his leadership style, and he was getting nowhere in his supervised ministry experience, even though he had been a very efficient leader in the army.

Kevin had asked to do his supervised ministry with the staff of a large church, in order to experience the type of ministry he felt most suited to do. He took his place under the associate pastor and found himself involved in committee work, in training teachers, and in the general budgeting procedures of the church. Soon various members of the committees and some teachers began complaining to Kevin, his supervisor, and members of his lay committee about Kevin's tactics. Apparently, army training had deeply influenced Kevin, and he continued to function in an authoritarian manner. Try as he would, Kevin's abrasive approach to people only mellowed slightly during this early period, and he began questioning his call to ministry. Then, after four months of the experience, Kevin resolved that the best course for him was to leave the ministry.

In the meantime, Kevin's lay committee became more aware of his genuine gifts and skills in administration, and felt the church could benefit from them. The lay committee spent several sessions sharing with one another and with Kevin the times when they, too, felt as if they had failed in a task to which God had called them. As they reflected together on their common experiences, Kevin began to see the possibilities of using his talents within a church setting in ways other than those he had originally planned. Kevin and his committee also continued working on his leadership style. Since then Kevin has shared on many occasions that the hours he spent in reflection with his lay committee enabled him to complete his seminary training and become a minister of administration.

Allyson's Committee

As a young mother and a full-time student, Allyson had to follow her schedule rather rigidly. For her supervised ministry experience she took a position as assistant to the minister of education in a church of about two thousand members. Her major reason for going to such a large church was that she respected the exceptional work of the minister of education who was to be her supervisor. Allyson's talents and skills in the position increased quickly as she threw herself diligently into the ministry of the church. Her lay committee members were committed to do all they could to introduce her to the various aspects of the church. They wrote an article each month for the church newsletter sharing something about her work or family. They placed pictures of Allyson, her family, and her ministry on the Sunday School's bulletin board. They took great pains to introduce her to all the committee chairpersons within the church, and spoke of her in their other church meetings.

As the year passed, however, a rift between the minister of education and the pastor seemed to widen. Members of her lay committee had seen such tensions arise before. They knew of Allyson's relationship to the minister of education, and wisely advised her how to remain detached from the feud and still continue to be friends with both the pastor and minister of education. When the minister of education decided to leave the church for a different position, the lay committee members recommended Allyson as a candidate for that position. With the blessing of her mentor, Allyson has since served the church well as the minister of education.

Ted's Committee

Ted began serving as minister of youth and education in a church of no more than eighty members. Located in a small town about sixty miles from the seminary, Ted worked mostly on weekends, except for some Wednesday responsibilities. Because of the models he had during his teenage years, Ted believed that God was calling him into youth ministry. Two short months after Ted's arrival, the pastor left the church. Ted's lay committee members were very impressed with his abilities and recommended that he be asked to serve as interim pastor. The deacons approached Ted about his willingness to serve in this capacity. Having never pictured himself as a preaching minister and having only preached in that church once or twice, Ted declined the invitation. After hearing several candidates for the interim position and visiting again with the lay committee, the deacons decided that Ted was, indeed, the person they needed. This time they did not ask Ted, but informed him that they wanted him to serve in that position. With the confidence of his lay committee, Ted became interim pastor, only to discover his love for preaching and his joy in caring for the congregation in ways he had never anticipated. The following year Ted changed his degree program and redefined his goals to an area of ministry he had not anticipated.

Why Have a Lay Committee?

We are reminded in 1 Corinthians 12 that the people of God are gifted for the common good. As part of the priesthood of all believers, each of us is called to ministry, to reconcile the world to God. Therefore, you and your lay committee can strengthen one another, working together as you perform the duties in the ministry to which God has called you, not only in your church, but also in your homes, workplaces, schools, and neighborhoods.

Lay committees can be an important means for bringing together the perspectives, skills, and desires of clergy and laity. Opening one more avenue for the voice of God to speak to you through a group of lay people can be both an exciting and a frightening experience. Ministers are called to empower the laity to do their ministries. Is your ministry and that of your church enhancing the ministries of the laity in their lives and work? What clues will they give you to help you better enable them in their ministries?

You can give your group of lay members the freedom to empower you. Lay committees have changed lives, recognized talents, opened doors, revised attitudes, and called out new abilities in students just like you. A lay committee of five to seven people can help you to review your options, evaluate your skills, reflect on your ministry, and analyze your abilities. Their feedback can give you a more holistic view of your ministry. To miss this gift by neglecting to have a lay committee may mean that you will fail to gain some very important perspectives for your future ministry and fail to be supportive of other people in important ways. The lay committee is a forum in which the soul of a congregation can be opened to you in ways seldom offered the student minister.

How Do You Form a Lay Committee?

With the help of your supervisor or a permanent standing committee of the church (such as the personnel committee), you will select five to seven persons to form your lay committee.

Qualities of Good Committee Members

Your committee members should represent the *diversity* within your church or agency. Some committee members should be *supportive and nurturing* persons. In the committee there also needs to be some people who are *confrontational* and willing to point out shortcomings in order to allow both you and other committee members to grow and change. There should be some people who are *reflective*. A very important aspect of the committee's agenda will be to reflect with you on ministry events. Therefore, you need persons who are both able and willing to do reflection. (Training sessions for dealing with the work of lay committees are usually offered by your school. In these sessions the committee members will probably be taught to use at least one style of doing theological reflection.) You will also want to have people on your committee who are *willing to learn* together, to *think through issues* and consider the implications of acting on those issues as a group. You will likewise do well to have someone who understands the various areas of your placement setting, including both community and denominational aspects of your work. Those persons whom you select should be willing and able *to share both personally and spiritually* from their experiences. They should be willing to *listen and ask questions* that will encourage others to make their own decisions. Finally, and of major importance, you should have some members in the group who are *familiar with the Scriptures*. Not everyone, of course, will have all of these characteristics or be able to fill all of these roles. However, the presence of all these characteristics among your various committee members should provide you with a more holistic experience in supervision than you would have if they were missing. Accordingly, be as selective as possible in forming the lay committee. The better selections you make, the better the chance that real learning and growth will take place.

In an agency you will need to develop relationships with people who can provide caring and honest feedback about the way you are perceived by those persons with whom you work. You might consider a committee of staff members or persons who will help you discover the reactions of the constituency in which you are working and who will not isolate you from feedback.

Pitfalls to Avoid

You as a student might be tempted to select only persons who love you and would not criticize your ministry, but such a limitation would result in a very shallow and unproductive experience. Next, you as a student might be tempted to use a committee that is already in place, for example, a music committee, if you are a minister of music. Although members of this committee would probably know about music, their lack of diversity might stalemate you in other concerns which the lay committee is duty bound to face. On the other hand, you might be tempted to select such a diversity of people that nothing would get accomplished in the lay committee because no one could agree.

You might be stymied in your selection because you are unsure about the gifts and abilities of members in the congregation. At times like these, you may need to depend on suggestions from persons who know the congregation or constituency better than you. By sharing the criteria with your supervisor, a permanent committee, or other knowledgeable persons, you may be able to make more appropriate selections. The selection process is crucial, and your committee members need to feel that they play an important role. They need to sense that they have both something to offer and a right to offer it. In your setting you can probably assume that some people will already possess skills that will be helpful in the functioning of such a committee. For instance, those who are counselors or teachers may be accustomed to doing supervision and know how to facilitate the working process of a group. When you think about the process, you may be surprised at the resources that are available in your congregation or constituency.

Your school may have a policy about whether the supervisor or pastor serve on the committee. Whatever that policy may be, keep the lines of communication open between you, the committee, the pastor, the supervisor, and the church or agency at large. By acknowledging the committee members in worship or at appropriate meetings, the members of your community will have a way of becoming a part of your learning situation.

What Are the Functions of a Lay Committee?

Once the committee has been formed, it becomes a full partner in the school's supervisory team of those who are charged with preparing persons for ministry. That team includes the field supervisor, the student, the lay committee, the school, and the congregation, institution, or agency where you are serving.

Encouraging You

Your lay committee has been asked to perform certain functions. The first and foremost responsibility is to be *supportive, helpful, and encouraging* to you as a student in your particular placement, especially in times of discouragement, stress, and pain. Growth and change can be painful. Discovering from feedback the way in which others perceive your ministry may be traumatic. The cumulative effect of encountering difficult crises, helping parishioners find solutions to problems, resolving conflicts, visiting the dying, creating programs, or directing committees, often requires much more than you are physically, emotionally, or spiritually ready to give as a minister. In times like these the committee's ministry of encouragement and support will be especially meaningful.

At times there may be issues which are very difficult to confront. A supportive, warm atmosphere may not always provide space to address these difficult and painful struggles. At those times your committee may insist that you talk about personal struggles that interfere with your ministry. In order to be this vulnerable with one another, the group members will need to be open to sharing both their faith resources and those things which tend to get in the way of ministry. Supporting one another as you go through these painful times is a gift you can give to one another when it is done in a nurturing climate of trust.

Interpreting Your Ministry Context

In addition, lay committees are charged with interpreting the ministry context for you. Ministry always takes place in a context. Each context is unique. Your committee members need to help you understand the constituency and the circumstances in which you have been placed. They must also help those persons who are being served to understand your ministry and the programs in which you are involved. By encouraging communication and accountability between your committee and the constituency, expectations and needs may be met with greater ease.

As some have suggested, the lay committee is a living textbook. When your committee members reveal themselves to you, you are able to see in depth that which may have taken years to discern and which you may not have had an opportunity to discover anywhere else. They can show you what it is like to live in another person's shoes. Their sharing of their lives with you will open doors of insight needed for you to provide meaningful ministry to your committee members and to your congregation or constituency.

All parties on the supervisory team must also think of themselves as both teachers and learners. Each party has gifts to give and needs to be filled. As your committee members live out their ministry in the world, they have insights to teach you. Taken together, your committee members will have many years of experience from which to draw information, knowledge, and insight, as a gift to share with you.

Covenanting with You

The committee is to covenant with you in order to provide focus and direction for the work of the committee. This process of covenanting includes such details as negotiating the meeting times and place, writing objectives and identifying the roles and functions of the committee members in relation to you, the congregation, the supervisor, and school personnel. A covenant may include pledging confidentiality, listening to one another, giving positive and negative feedback in supportive ways, attending regularly, and sharing insights and experiences. Learning to build a covenant is another skill that is usually taught to lay committee members during a training session. This covenant is not the same as your **learning covenant**. Rather, it includes those things that you and your committee members promise to each other. This covenant should be reviewed from time to time to check the progress and growth toward those things that you have set out to do within the group. You need to give honest feedback to your committee members about how they are fulfilling the covenant since they are expected to give you honest feedback about your ministry with them.

Your committee members should also review with you the learning covenant which you, along with your supervisor and/or school personnel, have designed for the course. In this way, the members will be better able to help you become aware of the progress you have made in your areas of concern. The committee members may also assist you in designing the learning goals for the covenant since they are intimately aware of the needs and concerns of the church or agency in which you are ministering.

Reflecting Theologically with You

Theological reflection with your committee has great potential for bringing about real change and making a difference in your life and in the lives of committee members. As a student, you probably understand the process of theological reflection. Your committee members, however, may find the concept threatening. They may be unaware that they are in fact doing theological reflection when they ask such questions as: "Where do I see God in this situation?" and "What would God have me do?" By considering the meaning and purpose of our lives, we are engaging in theological reflection.

There are many possible ways of doing theological reflection. One method, which is included for your consideration, has been tested with lay committees and seminary students throughout North America by the Education for Ministry program of the Bairnwick Center, School of Theology, University of the South in Sewanne, Tennessee. This process begins with a ministry event that you bring to the committee either orally or in writing.

Study the material in the box on page 77. In light of this material, let's think about an example. Suppose one of your assigned responsibilities is to do hospital visitation one week each month. You may not enjoy such an assignment although you have come to recognize its importance. Therefore, you have decided to bring to the committee an event involved in your last hospital visit. Your ministry event reads:

> Mrs. Brown has been fighting cancer for the last year. She is now in the hospital and has been told that she only has several weeks to live. As I pulled into the hospital parking lot I could feel myself beginning to perspire. I walked up the stairs to the third floor, since that would take longer than riding the elevator. When I reached Mrs. Brown's hospital door, I rejoiced that it was closed because that said to me she did not want visitors. Therefore, I turned around and took the elevator downstairs.

The committee members would then be given the opportunity of asking questions to clarify the incident in their minds and to decide together what was the critical moment in the incident. Suppose it was decided that walking up the stairs was a crucial time. You would be asked how you felt as you walked up the stairs. What were the thoughts and feelings you had as each foot hit a step? You may reveal that you felt worried. You could remember saying to yourself, "I hope she doesn't want visitors today. The pastor will be coming to visit her tomorrow. I don't know if I have anything to say to her. What can I say to a dying person?"

At that moment you could tell them that you felt fearful, inadequate, and unprepared. In response, the group would share with you times when they, too, felt "fearful," "inadequate," and "unpre-

Box 5.1

Ministry Event

A. Student Incident

    1. Committee members hear or read your ministry incident. They help clarify the thoughts, feelings, and actions involved by asking questions until they understand clearly what happened, what you did and what significance this incident has for you.

    2. You and the committee members must decide what is the most important moment in the event. In this way the group limits their attention to one specific focus in the event and the thoughts and feelings connected with that focus.

    3. Committee members then share with the group incidents from their own lives in which they have experienced the same or similar thoughts and feelings.

B. Image or Metaphor

    1. Together you and the committee members develop an image or metaphor which captures and focuses the thoughts and feelings identified in the incidents. Such distancing allows the group to gain perspective.

    2. What perspectives on life are offered by the image and the incidents?

C. Christian Tradition

    1. The group explores biblical passages or occurrences from Christian history which speak to this metaphor and these incidents.

D. Implications

    1. What are the implications to be explored because of what the Scriptures say? What changes in understanding and/or behavior does this reflection process cause you to consider?

pared." Once everyone has shared their stories, you and the group should brainstorm (list words or ideas without comment or critique until everyone's ideas are spoken and recorded) images or metaphors which gather up all these feelings. From this brainstorming session you should then select an image with which to work. This process allows the entire committee to step back and gain perspective. It gives freedom for everyone to comment without feeling judgmental. For instance, a list of images like the following may be suggested:

Taking a test for which one is unprepared;
Facing a court-martial;
Watching from the shore while someone is drowning;
Standing before God on Judgment Day;
Seeing a house burn and hearing a crying voice from inside;
Entering a dark neighborhood to visit a poor family;
Confronting a large, vicious-looking dog on the way to school;
Going to your window and noticing someone being beaten.

The group then selects the image which best fits the thoughts and feelings described.

Suppose the group selected the image of someone drowning. The question is, "What perspective on life does this image offer?" Once that question has been answered the group begins to brainstorm biblical passages or incidents from church history which speak to the image and its perspective on life. Some biblical selections which may be recorded are:

Elisha showing his servant the army of angels that surrounded them (2 Kings 6);
The story of the disciples on a storm-tossed sea (Mark 6);
Jesus' final words to His disciples, "Lo, I am with you always" (Matt. 28:20, NASB);
Jesus going to the tomb of Lazarus (John 11);
The disciples' fears about Jesus leaving them abandoned and His sending the counselor (John 14).

From such a list which your committee members have brainstormed, one passage should then be selected and read. The questions which the group addresses are:

What view of life does this passage of Scripture offer? What implications does it have for the original ministry event? What do these implications suggest for your future attitude and behavior?

Various methods for doing theological reflection are discussed in books such as Thomas H. Groome's *Christian Religious Education: Sharing Our Story and Vision*,[1] Evelyn Eaton and James D. Whitehead's *Method in Ministry: Theological Reflection and Christian Ministry*,[2] Joe Holland and Peter Henriots' pastoral circle in *Social Analysis: Linking Faith and Justice*.[3] (Also see chap. 8 for additional information on theological reflection.)

Whatever method is chosen for doing reflection, it is important that Christians seek to make sense out of God's presence in their lives. This task is everyone's responsibility. A lay committee is a strategic place to work together on such a significant process.

Evaluation

The final responsibility of the lay committee that should be mentioned here is evaluation. It is, however, not something that is accomplished by submitting a report once or twice a year. The lay committee should engage regularly in evaluation. Evaluation should become a natural part of the regular meetings. Both the content and process of each meeting should be evaluated. You will also want to evaluate the expectations and goals set forth both in the covenant that you and your lay committee wrote, and in your learning covenant that the field education director has approved. Evaluation is appropriate on both a formal and informal basis. Committee members should review what has happened at each meeting to determine if all is proceeding well, if anyone's behavior has interfered with the functioning of the committee, and if anything was overlooked or avoided in the content and process of the

1. Thomas H. Groome, *Christian Religious Education: Sharing Our Story and Vision* (San Francisco: Harper & Row, Publishers, 1980), 206–32.

2. James D. and Evelyn Eaton Whitehead, *Method in Ministry: Theological Reflection and Christian Ministry* (San Francisco: Harper & Row Publishers, 1980).

3. Joe Holland and Peter Henriots, *Social Analysis: Linking Faith and Justice* (New York: Orbis Books, 1983); for further resources see Kenneth Pohly, *Transforming the Rough Places: The Ministry of Supervision* (Dayton, Ohio: Whaleprints, 1993), 135–59 for an excellent bibliography.

committee's conversations. In this way both you and your committee members can gain new perspectives and make adjustments that are necessary for growth and change.

Giving feedback is the first step in the evaluation process. It involves the giving of data, the sharing of facts, and the temporary suspension of judgment. By offering the facts as they are experienced by the person sharing, feedback should not become a critique of defects, but rather it should offer you a larger perspective on your actions than you would normally have. It should create a climate of trust rather than defensiveness. One way of giving feedback which tends to create trust involves giving it from an "I" point of view. To give this kind of feedback, a person should describe the action that occurred and the way he or she felt or is feeling. Focusing the feedback on the personal feeling level rather than placing blame for the actions facilitates the processing of emotions. Check to see if the person receiving the feedback understands the message and if other people within the group have experienced similar or different reactions. By checking with others in the committee, the appropriateness of the feedback can be insured. Using good feedback practices allows both you and committee members to be less defensive and more open to growth. The lay committee should be inviting feedback from you as well as giving feedback.

The committee should be evaluating issues which reflect deep concerns, such as purpose, identity, personal authenticity, accountability, and authority, rather than scrutinizing your every activity. Evaluation should allow you to discover your strengths and weaknesses as you attempt to attain your goals and grow to your full ministry potential. Of course, the lay committee is also responsible for presenting to the school, in whatever way required, written evaluations of your ministry and how it is being perceived. Before the evaluation forms are submitted to school personnel, the committee will want to share with you the results of their deliberation. Evaluation in various forms is a significant part of the lay committee's task throughout your time together.

What About an Agenda?

You and the chairperson of your lay committee are responsible for creating an agenda, to give direction to each meeting. The committee members will be assisting in the process as together you evaluate at the end of each session. In this way evaluation helps to determine those things which need to be explored in future meetings.

The uniqueness of each committee makes suggesting a standardized agenda an impossible task. There are, however, some items which should be addressed early in the life of the committee. These items include having each person on the committee share his or her spiritual journey, creating a covenant between you and the committee members, and reviewing your learning covenant for the course. A ministry event should be included in the agenda of each session. Support from committee members and feedback about your ministry with them should also be a part of each agenda. A short devotional time may be a part of the regular committee meetings. The leadership for the devotional times may be shared with those persons willing to participate. Creating each agenda, however, should grow out of the committee's work and functioning.

As you prepare to end your relationship with the church or agency, talk with your lay committee about the process. Transitions are important. The way in which you say "goodbye" will help to prepare the way for the one who will follow you.

What Is Said by Persons Who Have Experienced the Lay Committee Process?

A Variety of Opinions

One student said, "Getting six or seven opinions on your ministry is very, very helpful. I'd go as far as to say let lay committees replace the supervisors. It's so much better to get more than one person's opinion. No matter how unbiased a person tries to be as a supervisor, he or she still is always going to be biased. If you are getting six or seven opinions it's so much better. One may give you a biased view and the next person probably will give you the opposite point of view, then others will probably try to balance it all and find a happy medium. I'd rather have a committee than one supervisor."

Constructive Criticism

A lay committee member said, "We all bared our guts to each other on all issues. We all shared expectations and were concerned for one another. . . . We helped [the student] understand that not everyone will give him strokes. He was very receptive to us, not a bit defensive. He took constructive criticism well. He recognized the places where he fell short and he worked on them."

Time Well Spent

Another lay person said, "I don't know of any time our lay committee came away feeling that they had wasted their time. The majority felt at first like 'Gosh, I don't have time to crowd this into my schedule,' but when they left they would say, 'I'm really glad that I came.' It speaks well of what was done."

Lay Perspective

A supervisor said, "It was helpful to the student to hear lay peoples' perspectives and to get in touch with their needs. It helped our student to understand where they are coming from in dealing with issues in the marketplace every day. The seminary sends students out with their own agenda and assumptions. Students decide what people need. We are often missing the lay people. We are not feeding them, not scratching where they itch. Church is certainly a place to come to hear an inspiring sermon and to study some Bible material, but is it too much to expect that it will be relevant to where the laity live and work? If we can get students in touch with lay people at that point, students can go out to serve with their antennas up (if you will) and be much more sensitive to where lay people are hurting and needing to grow."

One supervisor admitted, "I wish I had this exposure in seminary. The interaction with the laity is invaluable."

Theological Reflection

Concerning the use of theological reflection, one student said, "It took our meetings off of a superficial realm and automatically carried them a couple levels deeper . . . We dealt with some pretty significant issues in life. . . . Theological reflection may be the most beneficial thing that happened. If lay committees did that and nothing else, it would be a super experience with everyone involved."

A supervisor gave the following comment about theological reflection, "The best thing we did was theological reflection. It really provided opportunities for the student to get exposure to the way lay people think and provided lay people with an opportunity to get exposure to the way staff and students think."

Helpful Without Major Problem

One supervisor reflected that, "There were meetings when she really felt that there was no need for this, but she enjoyed meeting with the committee even though she didn't have any agenda to bring. Almost without fail the committee would get into areas that would push her to look at her ministry or look at her relationships, so that every meeting was beneficial, even if she did not have an agenda or there wasn't a major problem."

Eased Transition

A music student who was resigning as minister of music from a church he had served for several years said, "With the resignation process the committee was very helpful, very insightful. They told me some things I had never thought about because I had never discussed [them]. . . . They told me what they would want an individual who was resigning to do. I felt very comfortable. I'm glad we did it."

Of course, not everyone has had such a good experience. But by following the suggestions given in this chapter you have the possibility of developing new insights about yourself and the Christians with whom you serve, insights which are not readily available in many other places. Even if lay committees are not required in your supervised ministry program, why not try establishing one anyway? You probably will be surprised at the benefits that will accrue to both you and the people whom you seek to serve. May God bless you as you prepare for your particular ministry.

6

The Supervisory Conference

Paul Stevens

Supervision has been defined as "a method of education designed to effect those personal changes which will permit the integration into practice of self-understanding, relevant theory, substantive knowledge, and functional skills."[1] The **supervisory conference** offers the **field supervisor** the opportunity to discuss with the student how this integration is being effected in his or her life and ministry. William Pregnall has described the supervisory conference as the "the heart of Field Education." He states that "it is here that **field work** can become Field Education."[2]

The supervisory conference offers the supervisee an opportunity to ask "why" as well as "how" about ministry. The conference serves as a means of clarifying issues. Ministerial identity can be more clearly defined in dialogue with the supervisor. Although there may be no clear-cut answers to issues that arise, the supervisory conference provides an opportunity for dialogue and reflection about such issues.

The supervisory conference needs to be a regularly scheduled meeting that both you and your supervisor regard as sacred time. Your normal supervisory conference should be held weekly and last one hour. It is important to choose a setting where both you and your supervisor feel comfortable. Meeting in the pastor's office could bring to the conference unconscious issues of authority that inhibit relaxed and open conversation. It is important to choose a setting where you will not be interrupted. It may be feasible to choose a setting at the church or agency which is neutral ground. The key is to choose a time and place that allows for open discussion of your personal and ministerial issues. Leave matters related to the ministry of the institution for staff meetings. The supervisory conference focuses on your development.

This chapter discusses the roles of the student and supervisor in the supervisory conference, modes of supervision, characteristics and stages of the supervisory relationship, and elements of a supervisory conference. I hope that this overview of the supervisory rela-

---

1. Charles R. Feilding, *Education for Ministry* (Dayton, Ohio: American Association of Theological Schools, 1966), 228–34.
2. William S. Pregnall, "Supervision of Theological Students," vol. 1 of *Theological Field Education: A Collection of Key Resources* (ATFE, June 1977), 150.

tionship and conference will prepare you to take advantage of this valuable opportunity.

The Student's Role

You will need to assume a proactive role in the supervisory relationship. The supervisory experience is designed to help you prepare for ministry. You need to play an active role in your supervisory experience, taking responsibility for what you learn about yourself and about ministry. A positive attitude toward the supervisory experience will help to create a positive learning environment for you, your supervisor, and the people with whom you will be working.

Exercising Initiative

Your school will have requirements about the number and length of supervisory sessions. It will be your responsibility to see that these sessions occur, and that items you bring for consideration in the conference are covered.

You and your supervisor need to prepare for each meeting. Your school may require reports or assignments that must be reviewed before submission to the field education director. Your part of these reports should be completed before each conference so that your supervisor can have enough time to review them and return them. Failing to prepare for each supervisory session wastes time and energy.

Before arriving at the meeting you should make a list of issues you need to discuss. These may include events that have occurred since the last meeting that you want to report and discuss. You may want feedback from your supervisor's observation of your leadership, or you may want to discuss personal issues that have arisen from your experiences in the **placement**. You will definitely want to talk about progress on the **learning covenant**. If you have a good idea of the things you need to talk about before the conference, you can help insure that your supervisory needs are being met. Your supervisor cannot read your mind, so it is very important that you communicate clearly the items you want on the agenda.

You will need to exercise initiative in the supervisory relationship. There may be times when your supervisor is not providing as much feedback as you would like. You may feel that the feedback you are receiving is always positive and never helps you see areas for improvement. You may need to talk with your supervisor about this so that the two of you can agree on the kind of feedback that is beneficial to you and the way you can best receive it. You will need to let your supervisor know that you need and want to hear the negatives along with the positives.

You may sometimes feel that your supervisor is not taking the supervisory role as seriously as you would like. Again, you will need to take the first step in talking with your supervisor about your supervisory needs. If you let your supervisor know how important the supervisory experience is to you, he or she will probably respond with a renewed sense of interest in you and the supervisory ministry he or she is providing for you.

Focusing on Personal Growth

In each supervisory conference, you and your supervisor will focus on your growth and development as a person and minister. If the supervisory experience is to be as beneficial as possible, you will need to be open and honest with your supervisor about who you are, what you are doing in the placement, what you are learning, and which rough edges you are attempting to smooth. Your ability to share yourself will be an important ingredient in the success of your supervisory experience.

The Supervisor's Role

Your supervisor, if working from a positive perspective of supervision, will use the supervisory conference as a time to encourage your personal and professional growth and development. In the course of your supervisory experience, your supervisor may serve as a listener, prodder, affirmer, confronter, or teacher as you bring to light the issues surfacing in your ministry experience. If the supervision occurs in its ideal state, the supervisor will also be a learner as you teach through your experiences. Supervision is a two-way process: student and supervisor learn and grow when both parties take seriously their roles and responsibilities.

Supervisory Styles

A variety of supervisory styles exists. Every person, based on personal experience and learning style, will approach the supervisory relationship differently. Donald F. Beisswenger of Vanderbilt University has identified seven modes or styles of supervision.[3] In your supervisory experience you may encounter only one of these styles. Your supervisor will probably use several styles, but one style will predominate. Beisswenger has identified each style, including the primary goal of the style, the supervisor's tasks, the place upon which attention is focused in the supervisory relationship, the nature of the relationship, and the person in control of the relationship. A review of the seven modes follows.

1. *Work Evaluation Mode.* The supervisor is in control. The supervisor assigns tasks to the student; the student's goal is to accomplish the assigned tasks. The supervisor's role is to identify the student's work responsibilities and to evaluate the student's performance related to these responsibilities. Theological reflection and discussion about issues unrelated to the assigned tasks probably will not occur.

2. *Instructor Mode.* Here again, the supervisor dominates. The supervisor's primary role is to determine what the student needs to learn in order to become a competent minister. The supervisor, after determining what the student needs to learn, decides how the student will go about learning it and then evaluates the student's performance based on the supervisor's definition of ministerial competence. Attention in this type of supervisory relationship is placed on whether or not the student is learning what the supervisor deems important.

3. *Apprentice Mode.* In this mode as well, the supervisor controls the supervisory relationship. Supervisors who use this style of supervision will seek to teach students the skills of ministry by having the students observe and mirror them as they do min-

---

3. Donald F. Beisswenger, "Differentiating Modes of Supervision in Theological Education," *Theological Education*, ed. Jesse H. Ziegler (Vandalia, Ohio: The Association of Theological Schools, 1974), 50–58.

istry. The supervisor's primary task is to go about ministry while the student "tags along." As a result, the focus of attention in the supervisory experience is on the supervisor's completion of ministry tasks, not on the student's hands-on learning experience.

4. *Training Mode.* This structured, educationally-oriented mode of supervision focuses on the student's development as a professional, using a contract to define the supervisory experience. The supervisor's primary task is to establish an environment in which the student can grow and develop personally and professionally. Although control in this style of supervision is more balanced than the three previously described modes, the supervisor is still the dominant person in the supervisory relationship.

5. *Resource Mode.* The amount of control in the relationship is based on the initiative of the student. In this style, the supervisor views the task of supervision in a very loose manner, serving as a resource person when called upon by the student. The student is given responsibilities and is allowed to approach them without direction from the supervisor. Attention is placed on the resources available to the student to assist in the performance of ministry.

6. *Consultative Mode.* The primary goal of this mode is to help the student learn to clarify goals and solve problems. The supervisor's task is to work with the student in determining what the student wants and needs to learn, and to assist the student in this learning by consulting with the student about the ministry experiences. Supervision will be given based on what the student outlines as learning needs and expectations, and what kind of help the supervisor agrees to give the student. The supervisor may serve as a sounding board or may gently nudge a student toward a difficult area, encouraging the student to face the issue and work to solve it. In this style, the primary focus of control rests with the student, while the supervisor facilitates and encourages the student's ability to wrestle with the many issues and problems that may arise from the student's placement.

7. *Spiritual Guide Mode*. An increased awareness of God's revelation in the world as a result of reflection on ministry experiences is the primary concern of this style. The supervisor's tasks focus on reflecting with the student on day-to-day **ministry events** and seeking the theological implications of these experiences. Most of the attention in the supervisory relationship will be placed on the various people and events encountered in the student's ministry experience. This style of supervision is marked by a more equal approach as both supervisor and student seek to be aware of God's work in the world.

Seeking a Balanced Approach

Your supervisor may use a variety of these styles. One style, however, may be the preferred or dominant style. The most beneficial styles of supervision are those in which the student is given some control in the supervisory relationship. Therefore, the Training, Consultative, and Spiritual Guide modes would be preferable. You need to be aware of the variety of styles that can be used in supervision. Your initiative can have a great effect on the quality of your supervisory experience. If you feel that your supervisory relationship is more supervisor-controlled, talk with your supervisor and seek to incorporate a more balanced and collaborative approach to the supervisory task.

Four Characteristics of a
Healthy Supervisory Relationship

Several characteristics promote learning and growth in the supervisory relationship. Let's consider four of these characteristics: freedom, trust, honesty, and self-awareness.[4]

Characteristic #1: Freedom

Anxiety develops when a person feels in danger of being overexposed. The atmosphere of the supervisory relationship should reduce anxiety and increase the freedom to take risks. There should

---

4. The original idea for these basic elements comes from a lecture delivered at Southwestern Baptist Theological Seminary by Joe Gross on "Student-Supervisor Relationship" on October 6, 1974.

also be a freedom to love and be loved. Love is a force that binds. You and your supervisor will need this bonding, but you will also need freedom to experience anger and frustration. Some negative feelings will come to the surface during the supervisory conference, and they need to be expressed. The supervisory relationship should afford both the supervisor and student an opportunity to laugh at themselves. All of us make mistakes and "goof up." We need to be allowed to laugh at ourselves—not to take ourselves too seriously. Freedom to be yourself increases when you are able to reveal yourself and experience acceptance. For the supervised ministry experience to be most helpful, you must feel the freedom to be yourself.

Characteristic #2: Trust

You and your supervisor need to develop a sense of trust between yourselves. Trust involves believing that your supervisor has your best interests in mind and will not intentionally harm you. It includes being willing to be open and honest about yourself, your motivations, and your style of relating to others. At times the supervisory relationship will be strained. You will pass through these difficult moments more easily if you and your supervisor begin by agreeing to be open and truthful. Trust will make possible the sharing of both positive and negative thoughts and feelings that arise during the supervisory experience.

Characteristic #3: Honesty

Your supervisory relationship requires a special kind of honesty— honesty involving tact, timing, and common sense. This honesty should not take the form of vindictive judgment. Problems can arise when you or your supervisor fail to share your opinions or feelings honestly. A trusting environment will help you and your supervisor share honest feedback and evaluation. Even so, conflict sometimes arises. "Confrontation is often the caring response in the face of resistance. What counts is the method and purpose of confrontation. Honesty is crucial; to speak the truth in love is a Christian act. Mutuality requires that one hear the truth as well as speak it."[5]

5. Kenneth Pohly, "The Distinctiveness of Ministry Supervision," vol. 10 of *Journal of Supervision and Training in Ministry*, 1988, 123.

Characteristic #4: Self-awareness

You and your supervisor need to be in touch with your own feelings. This will provide the freedom for each of you to be aware and sensitive to the feelings of the other. Supervised ministry experiences provide a chance for you to explore your motivations and to increase your self-awareness.

A supervisory relationship characterized by freedom, trust, honesty, and self-awareness lays the foundation for a challenging and productive experience. It will be important that you assume responsibility for developing and maintaining these qualities in your supervisory relationships.

Three Stages of the Supervisory Relationship

The supervisory conference is part of the larger supervisory relationship. This relationship normally passes through three rather distinct phases. Let's examine these before discussing the weekly supervisory conference.

Stage #1: Initiation

The initiation stage serves as the foundation for all that will occur in the supervisory relationship. This stage involves getting to know your supervisor, negotiating your placement, clarifying expectations, and a rite of initiation.

Getting acquainted. The supervisory relationship is dependent on the development of truth, honesty, and openness. Sharing your pilgrimages is a good way to begin a nurturing relationship. You will want to talk about significant persons and events that have shaped you as a person and minister. At this beginning phase, it is normal for you to be tentative as you share significant parts of "who you are." As your supervisor handles these sacred parts of "who you are" in a responsible and caring way, you are building a basis for vulnerability and openness in the relationship.

Clarifying and establishing expectations. Most of us enter relationships with expectations and assumptions. It is important that you and your supervisor talk about the expectations you bring to the relationship. Both of you will need to clarify what you expect of the placement. A clear **learning/serving agreement** (or supervisory agreement) may save both of you hurt and disappointment as you move through the supervisory process. If you are timid about voicing your concerns, this may be a good opportunity to begin developing assertiveness. The supervisory agreement will cover details of your placement. The learning covenant will establish the learning goals, and means of evaluation.

Rite of initiation. It is important that the church or agency you will be ministering through formally recognize the ministry you are performing. This may be as elaborate as a formal installation service or as simple as an introduction and prayer of dedication.

Stage #2: Task

The bulk of the supervisory relationship is the ongoing process of supervision. This includes the routine supervisory sessions, when the focus is provided by ministry reports. Your verbal and written accounts of ministry events will be discussed and reflected on, in order for you to learn more about yourself, about being a minister, and about doing ministry. The learning covenant will be a regular part of the conference as you report on your progress.

The supervisory relationship is intended to provide structure which will enable you to succeed and meet your goals. Some supervisors may view the supervisory conference as an opportunity to critique your performance in the ministry setting. Whereas this may be an element of the conference, it is by no means the sum total. The supervisory conference should be a time when attention is focused on your practice of ministry, interpersonal skills, emotional responses, and sense of call to the ministry.

Stage #3: Closure

As your supervised ministry experience comes to an end, it is important to bring closure to your relationship with your supervisor.

Evaluation. While you have been receiving informal evaluation or feedback throughout your placement, the completion of your placement is an opportunity to formally evaluate your ministry performance, your major accomplishments, and your learning experience. Two primary instruments are your learning/serving agreement and your learning covenant. These documents state what you intended to do and learn during your placement. Use them as you evaluate the experience. Your school may also have a final evaluation form to use in this process. Ask for and expect to receive your supervisor's honest assessment.

Transition. The supervised ministry experience may be the first time you have been involved in an intense supervisory relationship. During the process, you have shared significant parts of your past, analyzed your ministry experiences, and clarified your calling. It is normal for students and supervisors to develop significant friendships. It is important for you and your supervisor to reassess and negotiate the kind of relationship you will have in the future.

Termination. Your relationship with your supervisor and your placement began with a rite of initiation. Now it is time to say good-bye. You may find it helpful to have a rite of blessing in which you commit the ministry you have been involved with into God's hands and receive a blessing from those who have nurtured and acknowledged your gifts. This can be a powerful experience, as you learn to trust God and others with a ministry in which you have invested, and you receive affirmation and confirmation from those who have observed your ministry.

Four Elements of a Supervisory Conference

Supervisory conferences involve one-on-one supervision. The issues examined in supervision are highly focused on your particular needs. Because of the personal and vocational issues that surface in the supervisory conference, an atmosphere of openness and trust is essential.

The supervisory conference should be a priority for both you and your supervisor. Your development as a minister is important. If your prospective supervisor is unwilling to make the commitment to meet weekly, find another supervisor! The supervisory conference is the time when you and your supervisor "hold up to the light pieces of behavior, moments in ministry by the student, and gently but steadily turn the experience so that, like a jewel, every facet can be examined."[6]

Early in the supervisory experience, conferences will focus on assessing your learning needs and developing a learning covenant. Most of the conferences throughout your placement will be

---

6. Pregnall, "Supervision of Theological Students," 150.

devoted to reflection on ministry experience. Toward the end of
your supervisory experience, evaluation of your growth and development as a person and minister will be the primary focus of supervisory sessions.

Supervisory conferences should address several issues:

- Professional skills—How can I do it?

- Personal identity—Who am I?

- Vocational identity—Is this for me?

- Theological reflection—Where is God in all this?

While your supervisory conference will reflect the distinctiveness you and your supervisor bring to the process, most conferences have a routine, even if it is never acknowledged nor intended.
I will describe a process that many find helpful.

Element #1: Reconnecting

When you meet with your supervisor, it is normal to begin each
conference by reconnecting. Reconnecting may involve discussing
the weather, current events, or events going on in your lives.
Reconnecting allows both of you to regain the rhythm and sense of
connection you experienced at the close of your last conference.

Element #2: Developing an Agenda

Each week you and your supervisor will need to negotiate the
agenda for the conference. Do you have a pressing situation that
needs to be discussed? Do you have a form or report to be completed in order to meet school requirements? The supervisor may
suggest a concern to be considered. Settle on an agenda that meets
both of your needs.

Element #3: Dealing with the Agenda

Most of the conference should be devoted to discussing issues
related to your learning. You will want to bring samples of your
ministry through **verbatim reports, journal** entries, ministry
reflections, **incident reports,** or **case** presentations. (See chap. 7
for a further discussion of data gathering.) These vignettes from
your ministry provide an opportunity for you and your supervisor
to look closely at how and why you do ministry the way you do.

As you relate these experiences, your supervisor will be listening to pick up indicators regarding not only the quality of the performance of ministry, but also the feelings you experienced. The supervisor might offer constructive criticism about performance and make suggestions as to how the ministry could have been done differently. Your supervisor might lead you to reflect on why you minister like you do and what alternatives you may have for future ministry opportunities.

Your supervisor should direct conversation toward your emotions during the event, and how these might have affected your actions. Perhaps your supervisor can assist you in naming emotions that influence you. There is always the possibility that you are bringing into the situation some baggage left from other experiences.

In the supervisory conference your supervisor will assist you in theological reflection. This topic will be examined in more detail in chapter 8 in this book, but it also should be mentioned in connection with the conference. Theological reflection "offers the means by which the connection can be made between spirituality and practice. . . . Its primary focus is on what happens at the intersection between what one believes and how one lives out that belief. Ministry supervision is concerned about the congruity between belief and practice. Theological reflection presses the question about where God is present in one's life to the implications for that Presence; it seeks to know how God's presence makes a difference in one's ministry."[7]

Remember that the primary focus of supervisory conferences is your development as a person and minister. Matters dealing primarily with the tasks involved in your job description might be more appropriate for consideration in staff meetings.

Element #4: Closure

As you conclude each week's conference, note unresolved matters needing further consideration. You may wish to give your supervisor feedback concerning ways the conference was helpful and note hindrances to progress. You should also seek and expect your supervisor's assessment of your progress.

---

7. Pohly, "The Destinctiveness of Ministry Supervision," 123.

Conclusion

The supervisory conference is a vital component of the supervisory experience. You and your supervisor must consider it important enough to faithfully schedule it into your weekly activities. Your openness to learning; your ability to relate effectively your ministry experiences, both in oral and written form; the relationship developed with your supervisor in these conferences; and the skills of your supervisor in providing supervision are all integral elements in positive supervisory experiences.

7

Tools for Data Gathering

William T. Pyle and Mary Alice Seals

What happens in supervised ministry? An experienced minister engages a student minister in a regular, structured conversation about the student's development and maturation as a person and as a minister. This conversation continues week by week throughout the **placement**. We have identified the process as an ongoing conversation. We have identified the goal of supervision as your development as a minister and person. In this chapter we will focus on ways to gather data from your ministry so that it can be brought to your supervision.

Mining provides a helpful analogy for the supervisory process. Doran McCarty insightfully develops this analogy: "A miner works a lode and brings samples to the assayer for him or her to analyze. In a similar way students bring their experiences to their supervisors, peers, and others, for evaluation. As an assayer breaks down the ore into various elements, supervision breaks down experiences into various components: compulsions, motivations, skills, reactions, understanding and theology."[1]

Throughout your supervised ministry placement, you will be bringing to supervision small samples of the actual **ministry events** you are experiencing. It is important that you bring accurate samples to supervision. You may be tempted to "doctor" the samples so that you are seen in a more positive light. If you yield to this temptation you will not have an accurate assessment of your ministry experiences. In order for you to truly benefit from supervision, you must be willing and able to trust your supervisor and you must desire to have your supervisor's insights and assessments of your ministry samples. Often students are surprised when others recognize value in their ministries which they had never seen. It takes courage to place vignettes from your ministry out in the open for a more experienced minister to assess. This can be a very effective means of learning about yourself and doing ministry.

Supervised ministry experience uses **data-gathering** in two distinct ways—in the **supervisory conference**, and in **peer reflection groups**. We have already discussed the supervisory conference. Many schools also use peer reflection groups as a part of the process in which students engage in peer supervision of each others' ministry experiences. We will begin our discussion of the various methods of data-gathering with a discussion of the **case study method** and its use with peer groups. Then we will discuss some other

---

1. Doran McCarty, *Supervising Ministry Students* (Atlanta: Home Mission Board, 1986), 10.

approaches to data-gathering that are often used in supervisory conferences.

Tool #1: Case Method

Case studies are particularly useful with small groups of students engaged in peer supervision. In this section we will provide an orientation to the case method, give suggestions for writing a **case,** and describe its usage in a peer group.

What Is the Case Method?

The case method "is a means of teaching and learning by the analysis of actual events."[2] The method was developed and used by Harvard Law School and Harvard Business School as a means of teaching students to make decisions by analyzing real cases. In the 1970s the Case Study Institute was begun and a concentrated effort was made to use the case method in training ministry students. Since then hundreds of seminary professors have been trained in its methodology.[3]

A case is a written description of an actual event in ministry where a decision must be made. The reader enters the event and vicariously experiences the tension.

Writing a Case

A case is written through the eyes of one person, and presents the reality that person experienced. A good case provides a concrete event where the major character faces a dilemma. Often cases focus on common, ordinary issues that ministers face. It is not necessary for you to have an extraordinary event in order to have a good case. In order to protect the identity of the persons involved, it is necessary to disguise the institution and persons involved. A case should be written in the third person and in the past tense. It is important to provide the necessary background information so that the persons reading your case can understand the dilemma. As in any good

---

2. Alan Neely, "Cases: What They Are and How to Study Them" (New Haven, Conn.: Case Study Institute, distributed by Yale Divinity School Library, 1978 and 1990), 1.

3. For more information on the Case Study Institute, contact the Association for Case Teaching, P. O. Box 243, Simsbury, Conn., 06070.

story, you will need to develop the major characters. Provide information about their backgrounds and significant relationships or conflicts.

Once you have selected a ministry event to use in your case study you are ready to begin organizing the material for your case. We suggest that you organize the material into four sections—Introduction, Background, Development, and Summary.

Introduction. Begin your case with a statement of the dilemma and a hint at the various alternatives available to the key participant. Let your readers know immediately the decision that must be made. It is essential that your case focus on the decision to be made.

Background. Provide the necessary background material including factual information about persons and events. Try to be objective and not make judgments concerning the motives of others. The background material sets the stage for the development of the plot.

Development. The central issues of the case are unfolded in the development section. You will include actual conversations among the participants, and actions that were taken. Describe your actions and involvement in the process. What did you (the major character) do, say, and think? It is important to organize the material so that the reader has a clear understanding of the chronological sequence of events involved. The development section should lead up to the dilemma and decision to be made.

Summary. Conclude the case at the point of the decision. Return to the original dilemma identified in the Introduction. The case ends with a question: "What do I do now?" Leave the case open-ended. You may have already been forced to make a decision by the time you present the case. If so, end your case with the dilemma you faced, and do not disclose the avenue you chose to follow.

Using Cases with Peer Groups

A peer group consisting of five to eight students provides an excellent opportunity for you to listen to others struggle with the dilemma you face. You may be surprised by alternatives suggested within the group, which you had not considered. As your peers discuss the situation, you may understand more clearly the perspectives and concerns held by other characters in the case. In some peer groups the case writer remains silent while the group discusses the case. You may be surprised what you can learn when you have to listen and are not preoccupied with defending your actions. As peer group members discuss the case, they develop and sharpen their diagnostic and problem-solving skills.

You can gain many insights in peer group case conferences. You will increasingly value collaborative learning. You will reveal your "functional" theology when you deal with real life events. You will discover that everyone does not operate from your frame of reference. You may even learn to appreciate and value the diversity of your peers.

Tool #2: Electronic Recording

With the rise in accessibility of recording devices, the use of electronic recordings in supervision has been made much easier. The use of audio recordings and especially video recordings in supervision is very beneficial, for it gives the student and the supervisor a concrete example of the student's leadership and interaction with others. As you remember your participation in ministry events, you may sometimes be guilty of "selective memory"— remembering things in the way you wish they had occurred. Audio and video recordings can help you to be more honest by demonstrating very objectively what occurred. Electronic recordings can also help you evaluate your physical or non-verbal communication, as well as the physical and verbal responses of the persons whom you were leading. Sometimes the opportunity of watching yourself from an objective viewpoint can help you see and hear nervous mannerisms and habits which you may not have been aware you had. Another benefit of using recordings in supervision is that the recording can be stopped, so that a particular item can be discussed before moving forward on the tape.

Yet using electronic recordings has its own pitfalls. Here are three words of caution for you.

Plan Ahead!

You may choose to record worship services, rehearsals, meetings, class sessions, and counseling sessions. Plan in advance to have the recording equipment set up and ready to go. If someone else will be responsible for running the equipment, make sure they know in advance what they need to do and when things should be ready.

Get Permission!

Secure the permission of those who will be included in the recording. In some settings, particularly counseling sessions, it is very important that you have permission to record the session. Explain to the persons involved why you are recording and how the recording will be used. Never record without seeking permission.

Be Yourself!

When cameras are rolling or tape is recording, you may be tempted to lead in affected or unnatural ways. Remember, you are using the recording to help you learn how you relate with and lead other people in ministry events, and how they respond to your leadership. If you "perform" for the recording, the value of getting at the real issues you must face will be minimized. Try to be as natural as possible when recording an event. You may also need to remind the persons being recorded that they must be as natural as possible. Some of them may choose to be on "good behavior," particularly if they feel you might be graded down because of their behavior. Let them know that you need for them to be themselves. If you relate to them in your natural manner, they will be more likely to respond to you in more natural ways.

Tool #3: Verbatim Reports

A **verbatim report** is a careful reporting of the conversation and metacommunications that occurred during a ministry event. Verbatim reports are commonly used in **Clinical Pastoral Education** and are particularly helpful when you wish to submit your communication for close and careful analysis. A verbatim report includes a transcript of the communication which occurred during the event. The transcript is written from your memory and it is understood that it is not as perfectly accurate as an electronic recording. Verbatim reports can be very helpful for analyzing transitional moments in conversation. Was there a place in the communication event where you were uncertain how to respond? Was there a place where you are not sure why you responded as you did or felt the way you felt? It is important to write your verbatim report as soon as possible after the event you wish to consider. We will suggest a format that has proven to be helpful in reporting ministry events.

Introduction

Provide background material which sets the context for the ministry event. Give pertinent information concerning the religious, social, familial, and psychological condition of the person or persons with whom you interacted. What was your state of mind as you entered the situation?

Transcript

Write a transcript from your memory of the communication event. Include not only the words spoken, but also body language, emotions felt or perceived, and actions. These can be included by placing them in parenthesis. Identify the speaker and movement by using notations in the margin such as P1, B1, P2, B2, P3, etc. Do not be overly preoccupied with providing a perfect transcript of the conversation. Do the best you can based on your memory of the conversation. Walter Jackson notes that "the way the event is remembered by the student is often more important for ministry learning than having the accurate transcript."[4]

Reflection

Identify the dynamics which occurred during the ministry event. What was happening with you, your interlocutor, or between you? Why did you choose to reflect on this event? What is the "rub" for you in this event? Where do you feel uncomfortable with the way the event turned out? At what point in the dialogue did you feel stuck, uncertain, frustrated, or afraid? What issues are unresolved for you?

Assessment

Assess your ministry in this event as it relates to process, skills, interpersonal dynamics, or the integration of faith and practice. What parts of this event can you affirm as effective ministry? What

---

4. Walter C. Jackson, *School of Theology Supervised Ministry Experience Manual: Instructions, Contracts and Report Forms* (Department of Ministry, The Southern Baptist Theological Seminary, 1994), 21.

parts do you wish you could do differently? What are you learning about yourself or your style of doing ministry? (See appendix 2 for a model verbatim report.)

Tool #4: Ministry Incident Reports

You may use an **incident report** to provide an account of a single event in ministry which has significance for you personally. Incident reports tend to be shorter than cases or verbatim reports. The report may include background of the incident, description of the incident, reflection on the event, and assessment of your ministry performance. This method of data-gathering may be particularly useful when you are needing to "unpack" an event which has a personal focus. Rather than focusing on what words you said during an incident, you may need to deal with your emotional response as you reflect on the event.

Tool #5: Process Notes

Process notes provide a different focus than the other means of data gathering discussed to this point. Cases focus on a decision that must be made. Electronic recordings allow the supervisor to hear and/or observe a ministry event. Verbatim reports focus on the conversation and metacommunications as you remembered and recorded the event. Ministry incident reports allow you to unpack a single incident which has personal significance for you.

Unlike a **journal**, which may cover a broad range of issues, process notes are used to consider a specific ministry issue over a longer period of time. For example, if you recognize that you have difficulty expressing your perspective when authority figures are present, you may wish to make periodic notations of incidents in which this was an issue. Process notes can also help you analyze a relationship as it develops over time. Where are the turning points? What caused the changes? Who initiated the changes?

The format may include similar categories as used with other methods of data-gathering. Set the stage by providing background material. Provide a chronological account of the development of the relationship or of incidents relating to the issue you are considering. You will want to give your reflections on the events which have occurred. It may also be helpful to reflect on ways this issue or relationship fits into the broader picture of your life and experience. You will want to conclude your report with an assessment of your growth and development through this experience. What have you learned about yourself? What have you learned about ministry? The longer period of time covered by a process note contributes to its value as a data-gathering method.

Tool #6: Journaling

While process notes allow you to keep a record of multiple incidents related to a common theme over a longer period of time, ministry journals allow you to make written reflections on a variety of issues you face throughout the supervisory experience. Some students may resist such a disciplined exercise. With care and consistency, however, keeping a running account of your experiences while in supervision can provide a wealth of material to further your growth potential while in the midst of supervision and beyond.

Writing about your experiences helps to clarify in your mind exactly what happened. Were you having trouble sorting through an incident? Writing about the incident in your journal may help you to unfold the dynamics of the event so that you can better understand what happened. Emotions that you may be afraid to vent openly may be more safely vented in your journal, perhaps providing you with the courage to follow your written words with appropriate spoken words. Writing about your ministry relationships may offer insight into your patterns of relating with others or may assist you in identifying new and effective ways of ministering to others.

A journal is not the same as a personal diary, in which you might record your deepest, most personal wants and desires. It is a tool for reporting the various activities you have been engaged in during your supervised ministry experience, and your thoughts and feelings about those experiences. A journal also provides a means of reflecting on your role in these experiences and your competence in dealing with various ministry issues.

Your **field supervisor** or your field education director may read your journal. Sharing yourself through your journal will require risk-taking and trust. Your honest and thoughtful journal entries can provide the basis for significant supervisory discussions if you invest the necessary energy to make the task meaningful.

Conclusion

In this chapter we have briefly surveyed some of the data-gathering methods used in theological field education. Your school will probably have guidelines and/or required methods that you will need to use. Each method has its own distinctive advantages and particular applications where it is most effective. Any of these methods can yield a wealth of self-understanding and growth. Regardless of which method your school uses, the critical elements in learning from experience are the same:

- Your willingness to place accurate samples of your ministry before your supervisor and peers;

- Your willingness to take seriously their feedback and questions;

- Your willingness to reflect on the issues raised by your ministry experience.

These tools for gathering data can provide a valuable resource for your growth and development as a person and minister.

8

Theological Reflection

William T. Pyle

What Is Theological Reflection?

Why Is Theological Reflection Necessary?

How Can You Do Theological Reflection?

The Whiteheads' Model of Theological Reflection
>   Christian Tradition
>   Personal Experience
>   Cultural Information

The Whiteheads' Method of Theological Reflection
>   Attending Stage
>   Assertion Stage
>   Decision-making Stage

Supervised ministry is field-based experiential learning. Beginning ministers involve themselves in ministry **placements** where they have the opportunity to function as vocational ministers. The process uses an action-reflection model: the students reflect upon actions in order to learn more about doing ministry and about being a minister. Experience without reflection is not education. Learning occurs when the student uses the experiences of ministry as a learning opportunity. This chapter will focus on the "reflection" part of the model, specifically **theological reflection.**

What Is Theological Reflection?

Critical reflection is the process of examining one's actions in order to identify the assumptions which are behind the actions, scrutinizing the accuracy and validity of the assumptions, and reconstituting these assumptions to include new insights, in order to make the assumptions more integrative of the experiences of reality. Assumptions are those "taken-for-granted ideas, common sense beliefs, and self-evident rules of thumb that inform our thoughts and actions."[1] Critical reflection is a normal and natural part of making sense out of life. It is the search for meaning and integration.

Theological reflection is "the search for meaning, when done in the light of faith."[2] Theological reflection occurs when the events of life are examined through the eyes of faith, in order to integrate experience and faith. This making sense of experience looks for God's presence and seeks to honor the insights gained from life. Theological reflection is the ongoing process of making sense of events as they occur. It is an over-simplification to think of theological reflection as only an action-reflection occurrence. It can be viewed more realistically as a repetitive cycle of action-reflection-action-reflection. Actions are reflected upon and the insights gained are integrated into subsequent actions, which are in turn reflected on again. This is a subconscious process which adults use daily. In supervised ministry courses, this process is raised to a conscious level and used intentionally to foster growth and integration.

Why Is Theological Reflection Necessary?

The simple answer to this question is that humans want the world to make sense. On a basic level, we long to clear up incongruences, inconsistencies, and ambiguities. Most of us struggle with the gulf between our longing to "make sense" and our recognition that reality does not fit neatly into our categories. Critical reflection is an attempt to move toward harmony and integration, an

---

1. Stephen Brookfield, "Using Critical Incidents to Explore Learners' Assumptions," in *Fostering Critical Reflection in Adulthood*, ed. Jack Mezirow (San Francisco: Jossey-Bass, 1990), 177.

2. Regina Coll, *Supervision of Ministry Students* (Collegeville, Minn.: Liturgical Press, 1992), 91.

attempt to examine assumptions in light of experience, an attempt to draw conceptual maps of reality which more closely match the terrain of life.

Cartography, or mapmaking, is at times an awkward and frustrating science. The cartographer attempts to produce a map or guide which provides an overview of the terrain. The map is never the terrain, however. By studying the map, a traveler can become familiar with distinctive features and can get a feel for how the land lies. But, it is still just a map. Skilled cartographers use the best data and instruments available to make their maps as accurate as possible. The more angles from which the cartographer can look, the less likely the features will be distorted on the map produced.

Like cartography, critical reflection looks at one's conceptual map of reality and explores angles that may have been overlooked. The goal of critical reflection is a more accurate view of reality that makes sense of the data.

Theological reflection uses all the data and angles of critical reflection, but looks through the lens of faith. Formal theologies contain propositional statements of assent. They are the maps of reality we formally affirm. Sometimes referred to as systematic theology, they are often expressed in creeds, resolutions, edicts, or statements of faith. Most of us inherit formal theologies from our churches, families, or significant mentors. Most student ministers come to theological education with an entrenched formal theology. They may or may not have reflected on it critically. In New Testament, Old Testament, and theology courses, new information is added to the mix. Sometimes student ministers find new insights, challenges, or confirmation for their formal theology. The process of examining assumptions and theologies under the light of new insights can be threatening, but it is a necessary part of growth and maturation. By the time you get to **theological field education,** you have probably already made adjustments to your stated theology.

In supervised ministry courses the actual practice of ministry often reveals a different theology. You express your functional theology through your actions, not your words. All of us have some discontinuity between our formal theology (what we say we believe) and our functional theology (how we live).

Ministry experiences provide concrete, specific incidents in which you reveal what you believe. This phenomenological approach assumes that your actions in particular events offer insights into your map of reality. Looking seriously at your ways of thinking and ways of acting can be disconcerting and bewildering. Trying to make sense of the world may seem overwhelming, but understanding why you think and act the way you do may be equally challenging. You have accumulated your assumptions through a complex assortment of education and experience. You may find it easier to master Hebrew than to get at the assumptions behind your actions. As difficult as Hebrew was for me to pass, it was easier than getting at my unquestioned assumptions. When questions spring from my actions, they are difficult to ignore.

- What are my assumptions about conflict which lead me to keep quiet about my opinions?

- How does my critical attitude toward others reflect my view of God, my parents, or my church?

These are not theoretical questions when they spring from specific critical incidents in my ministry. My actions reveal my theology. If I am going to be a person of integrity, I must be willing to look intentionally at my theology, as revealed by my actions, and examine what I believe.

Your experience in a ministry setting also provides additional information for your reflection. What is your experience teaching you about God, yourself, or ministry to others? Dan Aleshire suggests that when adults reflect theologically on the issues raised by the events of life, the constructed theology is far more relevant and deeply felt than propositions received and affirmed. He states, "when life provides the agenda for theology, theology ceases to be mere formal propositional thought and becomes the individual's attempt to interpret the rhythms of life in the presence of God."[3]

Some of the keenest insights you learn may be those you learn through experience. The comfort that comes from God's presence in crisis is a different truth learned in the emergency room of a hos-

---

3. Daniel Aleshire, *Faithcare: Ministering to All God's People Through the Ages of Life* (Philadelphia: Westminster Press, 1988), 163.

pital than the abstract truth learned in a classroom. Your experiences will provide significant information for your faith, and your faith will have an impact on the way you live.

How Can You Do Theological Reflection?

Theological reflection is reflection by a particular minister on a specific issue raised by a particular event in a specific context. While systematic theology may look at an issue in a theoretical (some might claim objective) way, theological reflection in supervised ministry is always done in a subjective way. The minister operates with a history, an experience, and a context. The process suggested is one you have probably already been using, but at a subconscious level. The process can be conceptually seen as a cycle of action-reflection-insight-decision-action. It may be used to make sense of a past event or to help you face a decision. Theological reflection can offer insight as you try to understand why you took the action you did. Or you may use the process to inform your response to a decision you must make. In either case, you will need to choose a **ministry event** in which you feel a "pinch," an uncomfortable feeling about your response. The written form of the event may be either a **case, verbatim report**, or **incident report**. The form is not so important as the fact that you are beginning with an event that raises questions.

The purpose of theological reflection is to use experience to inform theology, and to apply the insights of reflection to the practice of ministry. A number of approaches have been proposed to facilitate the process. The approach I have chosen to use as an example of theological reflection is developed by James and Evelyn Whitehead in their insightful book, *Method in Ministry: Theological Reflection and Christian Ministry*.[4]

The Whiteheads define theological reflection as "the process of bringing to bear in the practical decisions of ministry the resources of Christian faith."[5] The Whiteheads' approach to theological reflection is developed through a model and method.

The *model* identifies three sources of relevant information to be listened to as a pastoral decision is contemplated:

---

4. James D. and Evelyn Eaton Whitehead, *Method in Ministry: Theological Reflection and Christian Ministry* (San Francisco: HarperCollins, 1980).

5. Ibid., 1.

- Christian tradition,

- Experience,

- Culture.

Each of these threes provide insights for action.

The *method* of using the information to inform pastoral decisions also contains three components:

- Attending,

- Assertion,

- Decision.

One primary advantage of the Whiteheads' model for our use is the broad range of relevant information that is sought for insight. A primary advantage of their method is that it provides a vehicle for moving from insight to pastoral action. The final purpose of the reflection is not better understanding, but relevant response to the challenges of ministry. I will describe each part of the process and provide an abbreviated example of the kinds of questions to be asked at each stage. I will use the following **ministry event** for the example:

> I am the pastor of an urban-fringe congregation. Our Sunday morning worship service averages seventy-five in attendance. The church has always been a "family chapel" church consisting of a few extended families. The community has changed from a rural farming community to an urban-fringe community. New families in the community have begun attending our church. Their new ideas are challenging our old traditions. At times it seems like I am pastoring two separate congregations. The old families are opposed to change and the new families are asking, "Why do we have to do things this way?"

The issue I want to reflect on is this: How can I provide leadership to heal the division which is developing and lead the church to minister to this changing community?

The Whiteheads' Model
of Theological Reflection

When a pastoral decision is necessary, all relevant information should be sought for use in the reflection. I assume that you will already have assumptions about the "proper" course of action. You have been compiling information that informs your actions as you have studied, experienced, and reflected. During the process of theological reflection, it is necessary for you to suspend judgment and forget that you already know the "answer" to the decision you face. If you fail to suspend judgment, you are likely to receive only information that will confirm your assumptions. Reflection then becomes a process of accumulating support for the answers you already have. If you are going to be open to new insights, you must be willing to suppose that there is something yet for you to learn. One way to prepare yourself for the process is to be aware of your predisposition and to be open to information that challenges your prejudice. Once you have identified your predisposition and decided to search for relevant information, regardless of the outcome, you are ready to go to the three sources for the insights they can provide.

The search will probably not be neat and tidy. You will find information that can't be reconciled. Don't be concerned at this point, or try to make sense of it. If the information does fit into a neat package, you might ask yourself whether you are filtering out information that contradicts your assumptions. The Whiteheads use the term *pluriformity* to describe the diversity of information that is available.[6] This diversity offers a cache of information to be mined. Given these initial observations, let's begin by looking at the three sources of information.

Christian Tradition

Christian tradition includes insights from the Old Testament, New Testament, and the experiences of Christians as this issue has been addressed through the past twenty centuries. Tradition consists of those things handed down to us from previous generations. How has this issue been addressed either directly or indirectly? Does Scripture address this issue through exhortation, illustration,

---

6. Whitehead and Whitehead, 15.

or example? What paradigms are evident in Scripture? Does the life of Jesus offer insights through His words, actions, or attitudes? How have other Christians through the centuries experienced this issue?

Robert L. Richardson, Jr. has identified four levels of information found in Tradition: (1) sacred Scripture as a deposit of tradition; (2) the teachings and practices of the church through the ages; (3) your particular denomination; and (4) your particular congregation.[7] You will have to sift through a wealth of information in order to identify that which is relevant to the issue. The information you uncover will present various perspectives. Depending on the source, the weight you give to the information will be different. You probably already have a hierarchy of value for these different levels of tradition. You might want to look at the reasons you give a higher value to one level of Christian tradition than to another. In your congregation, the authority of Scripture may be the highest authority, unless of course it differs from "the way we do things around here." Your challenge will be to enlarge your information base so that you can make informed decisions in ministry. As you reflect on the issues in the examples mentioned earlier, you may ask yourself these kinds of questions as they relate personal experience to the issues raised by the ministry event mentioned earlier.

- What models of leadership can be found in the Old Testament?
- What models of leadership can be found in the New Testament?
- What models of leadership can be found in church history?
- Does Scripture address the issue of division in a faith community?
- What insights or possible solutions are suggested in Scripture?
- What models are provided in my denomination?
- What models have proven helpful in this congregation's history in times of crisis?

7.   Robert L. Richardson Jr., "A Method and a Model for Theological Reflection," unpublished handout for supervised ministry students and field supervisors, Southeastern Baptist Theological Seminary, 1984. I am indebted to Bob for his insightful application of the Whiteheads' method and model for supervised ministry students.

Personal Experience

Every minister approaches decisions in ministry with a personal history. You have already dealt with the issue at hand or one similar to it in the past. The enterprise of theological reflection began with your experience in a specific event in ministry. Now you need to examine ways you have experienced this issue before. What was the outcome? What were you feeling during the event? Where have you felt that way before? What is your bias or predisposition concerning this issue?

If your understanding of revelation contains an awareness that God continues to be present and operative in the encounters of life, you will need to be sensitive to the rhythm of self-revelation that God is employing in your life. This approach to theological reflection assumes that God's self-revelation continues as we open ourselves to new and fresh insights.

The term *experience* is used in theological reflection to refer to "that set of ideas, feelings, biases, and insights which a particular minister and community bring to a pastoral reflection. Experience thus embraces not only ideas or 'understandings' but a wide range of rational and extra-rational convictions, hopes, and apprehensions."[8] Your reflection will be richer and more relevant as you carefully look at the information you bring from your experience.

Not everyone appreciates this approach because it takes seriously personal experience. Some may be more comfortable keeping the focus on Christian tradition and keeping the issue theoretical. To do so is to risk not seeing the hand of God at work in your life. Experience is not an enemy of Christian tradition. Truth is valid whether the insight initially comes from experience or Christian tradition. The Whiteheads envision experience and Christian tradition serving complementary roles. Rather than leading away from tradition, experience most often sends the searcher back to tradition for clarifying insights. "Rarely does increased awareness of personal experience seem to lead Christians away from their Tradition: more often it leads them toward it."[9]

8. Whitehead and Whitehead, 53.
9. Ibid., 61.

Before leaving this discussion of personal experience, I want to point out the value of the experience of your community of faith as a source of information. You are not the only person with experiences that offer insights. Your theological reflection should not ignore the information present within the experiences of persons within your context of ministry. How has your congregation experienced this issue before? What is the bias within your community? What is the source of that bias? Take seriously your experience and that of your faith community as you reflect theologically. If you do not do so, your reflection will be abstract and disconnected from you and your context. Now study these questions as they relate personal experience to the issues raised by the ministry event mentioned earlier.

- What have I learned from past experiences of conflict?
- What style of leadership has been helpful?
- What bias do I bring with me to this situation?
- What styles of conflict management have I used in the past?
- What were the results?
- What is my normal reaction to this kind of situation?
- When have I been the defender of the status quo?
- When have I been the challenger of the status quo?

Cultural Information

Cultural information refers to all the data in one's culture that provides insight or understanding to a pastoral concern. It includes information from disciplines such as philosophy, political science, psychology, world religions, and sociology. Any information that helps us understand ourselves or our world is germane to theological reflection. For instance, developmental psychology offers significant insights into how persons think and learn at different stages of life. This is pertinent information to discussions of faith development or educational methodologies. Information from culture includes not only that which comes from organized disciplines, but also the axioms and myths of the culture. Don Browning describes culture as "a set of symbols, stories (myths), and norms for conduct that orient a society or group cognitively, effectively, and behaviorally to the world in which it lives."[10] What data are available to inform your decision? How can you gather the relevant data? How do you determine which information is relevant?

Ask yourself these questions as they relate cultural information to the ministry event described earlier.

- What can I learn about leadership from business management?
- What insight can family systems theory provide for understanding my church?
- Can developmental psychology help me understand how senior adults and young adults view change?
- What information is available on leading organizations through transitions?
- Is there any research that identifies what "normally" happens to congregations in crisis?

Your search will need to be broad enough and deep enough to gather all the information relevant to your concern. You are not likely to probe too deeply into one of these sources of information. More likely, you will become satisfied with the information you have and discontinue your search.

The Whiteheads' model focuses on identifying sources of information to use in theological reflection. We will now turn our attention to the method. How can the diverse information found in Christian tradition, personal experience, and culture be brought together in a coherent way in order to inform a pastoral decision?

The Whiteheads' Method of Theological Reflection

The Whiteheads' method of theological reflection provides a way for the pluriformity of information from Christian tradition,

---

10. Don Browning, *The Moral Context of Pastoral Care* (Philadelphia: Westminster Press, 1976), 73.

personal experience, and culture to be used in making pastoral decisions. The challenge for this method, as with any method of theological reflection, is to be able to take seriously all the information available. Often the information from one of the sources is slighted in the reflection. When reflection is simply a dialogue between Christian tradition and personal experience, and cultural information is slighted, the conclusions may be what the Whiteheads refer to as "fundamentalistic." When experience is slighted, reflection becomes theoretical. When Christian tradition is neglected, the conclusion will not be specifically Christian.[11] The Whiteheads' method is an attempt to give all three sources of information a voice in theological reflection.

Attending Stage

In order for a minister to hear or see (perceive) God's self-revelation or truth, the minister must be a listener. When you approach your task of theological reflection as a searcher looking for insight, rather than a possessor intent on protecting the truth, you are more inclined to listen and hear new insights. The Whiteheads use the term *attending* to focus on the necessary stance of a learner, which is, to pay attention. Perhaps in your academic preparation you have already taken courses that focused on effective communication between persons and groups. Active listening focuses on all communication processes: "the words and silences, the emotions and ideas, the situation in which the conversation takes place."[12] Ministers need to bring all their listening skills to the task of theological reflection.

This stage of the method involves actively listening to each source of information in order to hear the insights that may impact the pastoral decision. If you are willing to suspend judgment and approach the issue as a seeker, you will be able to discover a plethora of information. Look for information in unexpected places by using methods such as brainstorming. Where would you look for information if you started with a different set of assumptions, or with a different frame of reference? In this stage of the process, don't be too quick to decide that information is irrelevant to the issue. Your task at this stage is listening—not judging.

---

11. Whitehead and Whitehead, 96.
12. Ibid., 83.

> This first stage of the method involves searching the three
> sources of information identified in the model. Compile the
> insights gathered from asking the questions raised under
> Christian Tradition, Personal Experience, and Cultural
> Information.

Assertion Stage

When the information from the three sources has been gathered, the focus turns to the process of generating a clarifying dialogue between the sources. You will have information from various
perspectives that suggests diverse possible responses to your initial
pastoral concern. What do you do with the information now? The
assertion stage involves engaging "the information from these three
sources in a process of mutual clarification and challenge in order
to expand and deepen religious insight."[13]

Assertion is a style of interaction through which conflicting
information is brought into dialogue for clarification, challenge, or
confirmation. Recent studies on assertive skills and behavior provide the background for the use of the term *assertion* to name this
stage in the method. Assertive behavior is the middle ground
between non-assertiveness and aggression. The three sources provide information to be used to question and clarify other information. In an open dialogue, the three sources neither overpower nor
are overpowered by one another. Each stands as a vital source of
information and offers insights for pastoral decisions.

Sometimes the Christian tradition challenges the values of a culture. Sometimes personal experience raises questions about the
authenticity of a portion of Christian tradition. Culture often provides insights from the social sciences that enlighten personal experience and Christian tradition. Through the process of clarification
and challenge, you will gain insights to be used in the pastoral decision. All the information you bring to the dialogue will not be given
the same weight in your reflection. I place Christian tradition, par-

---

13. Whitehead and Whitehead, 22.

ticularly the witness of Scripture, as the highest authority in my reflection. It is important for you to be aware of the hierarchy of values you bring to the process.

Is there a source of information that needs "assertiveness training?" Is there a "bully" who intimidates and silences conflicting voices? Your task as "manager" of the process is to see that each source of information has a voice and is willing to grant a voice to other divergent sources of information. You are the referee who monitors the interaction. You will need to be aware of your tendencies to short-change the dialogue, or favor one source over the others. You may want to request the assistance of your **field supervisor**, **lay committee**, or peers in monitoring the balance in your reflection.

- Bring the information you have gathered into an active dialogue.
- In what ways do your past experiences with conflict correspond to what you have learned about conflict management?
- Compare leadership styles used in business management with biblical models.
- Is the information supplied by family systems theory consistent with your experience? In what ways is it similar or dissimilar?
- How does your information on the life cycle stage of senior adults and younger adults make sense of the views toward change among your congregation?

Decision-making Stage

The Whiteheads' method of theological reflection begins with listening to the three sources of information and then moves to an interactive dialogue between the sources of information. This dialogue moves beyond the collection of information to the discerning of insights. Up to this point in the process, the stages could have taken place in the academy. But this method does not stop with the critical assessment of information. The context for starting the process was a ministry problem, an event which raised issues.

In this final stage of the method, we return to your setting. As a minister, you do not have the luxury of leaving the issue undecided. You may wish that you could wait for more information (particularly if you score high on the scale of perceiving (P) on the Myers-Briggs Type Indicator). Ministers most often focus on pastoral situations requiring decision and action. Your listening to information and interacting with the information has probably not removed all of the fog and ambiguity from the issue, yet you must move through insight to decision, and on to action.

The movement beyond insight to decision opens the door for you to plan your pastoral intervention. How can your insights be translated into concrete action? I suggest these six steps:

1. Identify the pastoral concern. What is the issue that needs to be faced?

2. Envision goals. How can the future be different?

3. State your mission. What are the values your goals express?

4. Set the agenda. What are my options for proactive response?

5. Implement your strategy. This is my decision.

6. Assess your intervention. How will I know how well my strategy is working?[14]

Ask yourself these questions:

> * What am I going to do?
> * What do I hope to accomplish?
> * What course of action will be consistent with my goals and mission?
> * What are the steps in my proactive response?

These steps in the final stage of the Whiteheads' method provide a strategy for using the insights of theological reflection in the practical decisions of ministry. Your decisions will only be as

14. Whitehead and Whitehead, 104–11.

informed as you are willing to open yourself to new insights. If your primary need is to affirm the status quo, this process will probably not be worthwhile. If you are committed to doing the necessary reflection to learn all you can from experience and to move from insight to informed pastoral decisions, this process will provide a great opportunity for growth. The choice is yours.

9

Evaluation in the Supervisory Experience

Mary Alice Seals

Purpose

Who Are the Evaluators?

    Student
    Field Supervisor/Lay Committee
    Peer Group and Peer Group Leader
    Ministry Recipients

Modes and Manners of Evaluation

Issues in Evaluation

Learning and growth are key goals in the supervisory experience. Quality evaluation is one of the best ways to assure the attaining of these goals. In this chapter we will look at evaluation. Why do you need evaluation? What kinds of evaluation will you experience? Who will evaluate you? When will they do it? What methods will they use? What will they be looking for? This chapter should help you learn and grow through your supervised ministry experience.

Purpose

In the early days of ministry training, students were given opportunities to minister in the field. In many cases this was viewed as **field work** or field employment. Many schools required field experience primarily to let students try out ministry skills and earn additional income. Other ministry training programs encouraged students to provide ministry to the community through **field ser-**

vice. This community service allowed students to try on the role of minister, practice ministry skills, and gain valuable experience.

Both of these forms of gaining ministry experience were, and are, worthy—for we all know the financial hardships of student ministers and the desire to provide service to the community. These forms of field experience did not emphasize intentional learning and growth through the ministry opportunity. Certainly learning and growth were by-products of the experience. Ministry experiences would have been much more beneficial if students had received feedback from persons connected to the ministry experiences.

Our approach to field experience is called "supervised ministry experience." In supervised ministry (perhaps in a remunerative position and hopefully in one which provides a service to the community) the student gains experience while enjoying the benefits of quality supervision and evaluation. It is the intentional focus upon evaluation that makes supervised ministry experiences much more valuable and beneficial to the student. Therefore, the process of evaluation in the supervisory experience is crucial in order for the student to learn and grow as a result of the ministry experience.

Who Are the Evaluators?

In supervised ministry experiences there are many people affected by the work of student ministers who also participate in the evaluation process.

- Students are certainly affected by the supervisory experience, hopefully in positive ways as they become more comfortable with the role of the minister and the various skills and abilities necessary for effective ministry.

- Field supervisors are affected by the supervisory relationship—both as those who minister with students in the ministry setting and as those who minister to students through the provision of careful and thoughtful supervision.

- Lay persons may also be a part of the supervisory team in some settings. These individuals, too, are affected by the supervisory experience. As with field supervisors, the ministry of lay committees with and to students should have an impact not only on the students' lives and ministries, but also on the lives and ministries of the persons on the lay supervisory team.

- Ministry recipients are also affected by the ministry of the student and indirectly provide feedback.

- The student's peer group and peer group leader are also evaluators. They may not actually observe the ministry of the student firsthand, but they do learn of the student's views and attitudes toward ministry as the student relates ministry events within the peer group. They also learn firsthand how the student relates to different people as relationships are developed in the peer group experience.

All of these individuals are a part of the evaluation team. All except the peer group and peer group leader evaluate the student in the ministry setting. Some of these will provide explicit evaluation during formal times for discussion and evaluation. Others will provide more implicit evaluation. Their verbal feedback should serve as important data for determining the student's effectiveness. Just as important is the nonverbal evaluation they give through their attitudes, attendance, and enthusiasm.

A variety of persons are a part of the evaluation team: the student, the field supervisor, the lay committee, the ministry recipients, the peer group and the peer group leader. Do all of these individuals do the same kind of evaluation of the student's ministry experience? No. Nor are all of these individuals and groups charged with the official responsibility of evaluating the student. The benefit of seeking evaluation from such a diverse group of persons is that each can evaluate the student and the student's ministry from differing perspectives. Each of us views the world through different lenses. This variety of perspectives offers the student a more realistic picture of how he or she is viewed as a person and as a minister.

Let's take a closer look at the different individuals involved in evaluation, and at the variety of things they are evaluating in the supervisory experience.

Student

Many of us have a picture of who we are. This picture is often multifaceted: the person we think we are, the person we want people to think we are, and the person people think we are based on their impressions or experiences with us. One of the goals of supervision is to check our perception of who we think we are with other persons' perceptions. This requires that we have a good picture of who we are as individuals, including awareness of the good, the bad, and the ugly about ourselves. This does not mean berating ourselves for our weaknesses. It does mean, however, acknowledging the not-so-pretty side of ourselves and working to improve these areas, as well as learning to accept and acknowledge the good side of ourselves—our gifts and abilities. Recognizing the events that have shaped you both negatively and positively is a part of self-awareness which is essential for self-evaluation. Self-evaluation is a part of being a proactive person—taking charge of, and responsibility for, your life rather than letting others do the acting. Self-evaluation puts you at the helm of the learning experience and can increase your motivation for benefiting from the supervisory experience. This self-motivation can be an asset throughout your years of ministry.

As you evaluate your own ministry skills and abilities, you will also be evaluating the effectiveness of those ministering with you. As you observe and experience the leadership of fellow ministers, you can learn about styles of leadership, noting behaviors and outcomes of ministry leadership that may or may not be appropriate for you.

Evaluating the ministry setting and its appropriateness to your ministry skills and abilities will be a part of your supervisory experience. This type of evaluation can be especially beneficial if you are new to ministry and are not yet sure exactly what form your future ministry is to take. Trying on different experiences in the supervisory experience and evaluating those experiences in light of who you are and what you want to do in ministry, can be a helpful tool in determining which ministry best suits you.

As a student, you will also be evaluating your supervisor. Some of this evaluation may be tacit and informal. You may observe your supervisor's interactions with you and others, and learn from these observations as ministry is modeled for you. In a more formal manner, your school may require you to write an evaluation of the supervision provided for you in the ministry setting. You will be providing feedback for your supervisor in much the same way the supervisor is providing feedback for you.

As you progress toward attaining the learning goals established at the start of the supervisory experience you will be one of the primary persons responsible for evaluating your level of achievement. Others will help you in this process. You will know in a more personal way the effectiveness and value of the learning that has occurred in connection to your learning goals.

Your self-evaluation is an important facet of the supervised ministry experience. Do not go through this experience as a passive participant in the evaluation process. Take charge of your own learning. Take an active role in evaluating your own actions and motivations, while remaining open to the evaluation you receive from others. These opportunities can help you develop and enhance your life-long learning skills.

Field Supervisor/Lay Committee

The field supervisor and/or lay committee will be providing the primary evaluation during your supervised ministry experience. It is essential that the people you select to provide supervision for you are comfortable in evaluating you. As in self-evaluation, this means that they are capable of saying not only the good and easy-to-hear things, but also caring enough to tell you about the areas of your personal and ministerial identity that need improvement. Note that the term "caring" was used. The persons who evaluate you must care about you and they must care about the ministry of supervision they are providing for you. If you do not recognize this sense of care in them, it will be difficult for you to hear and accept the evaluation being offered.

In order to gather data to use as a basis for evaluation, it is best if your field supervisor and/or lay committee members are able to observe you in action. While it may not be appropriate for them to observe directly all of your ministry tasks (for example, your personal counseling skills), it is important that they experience your leading and interacting with others in the ministry setting. Video recordings, audio recordings, and written ministry reports can provide a good basis for evaluation of your ministry. However, firsthand observation is still preferred. As discussion occurs in the

supervisory conference concerning your ministry experience, it will be helpful if the supervisor or lay committee members can have a personal frame of reference for the ways in which you lead and interact with others.

The evaluation received from the supervisor or lay committee will include their personal perceptions and feedback related to your ministry. They will also serve as conduits of feedback from the congregation or ministry recipients. This triangular relationship, if handled properly and not abused, can be a useful source of information for you in the supervisory experience.

The supervisor and lay committee will also assist in the learning process by encouraging dialogue and questioning in the supervisory experience. Good supervision assists you in seeking the answers to difficult questions, rather than providing easy answers. Evaluation will help you over the rough spots—challenging you to look at the difficult parts of ministry, while supporting you in the process.

In the previous section on self-evaluation we looked at the various perceptions of the student (who the student *really* is, who the student wants to be known as, and how others view the student). The field supervisor and lay committee will help you with the third part of this. A significant part of the supervisory experience is the time spent in helping you see how you are perceived by others. Often your self-perception and others' perceptions of you differ greatly. It is the task of evaluation to raise the issue of the incongruence and explore ways to bring the two images closer together.

Your educational institution will require official evaluative reports from your supervisor and lay committee. The types of reports required will vary from one school to another. Nothing in these reports should be hidden from you. Nothing in these reports should be a surprise to you. If good, open, and honest feedback has occurred throughout the supervisory experience, these official evaluation reports will be no more than written accounts of the supervisory experience.

Since the evaluation provided by the field supervisor and lay committee is so important to the supervisory experience, it is very important that caring, qualified individuals be selected to fill this role. Take care in selecting persons who are comfortable with pro-

viding meaningful evaluation, and who will take the time and care
to communicate this evaluation to you.

Peer Group and Peer Group Leader

The individuals in your peer group, both your fellow students
and the peer group leader, can also be a valuable source of evaluation. These individuals will know firsthand what it is like to be a student in training for ministry. They will be able to give you feedback
as ones who are walking along beside you and as ones who have perhaps been in similar situations. As you relate to your peer group,
they can help you see how your self-perception relates to their perceptions of you. This can only happen if the group is committed to
making it happen—if caring and risk are present. The peer group
facilitator also has a lot to do with the probability of this happening.

Your peer group will evaluate **ministry events** you share from
your field experience, and your actions in dealing with these events.
If your group uses **case** studies, you will be receiving evaluation
from the group based on the data you share with them and the dialogue that follows. Evaluation will also occur based on the ways in
which you relate to the other peer group members and the peer
group leader. Some supervised ministry programs require peer
review at the conclusion of the supervisory experience. At this time
verbal and/or written evaluation may be shared in relation to your
participation in the learning process and the group process. This
can be a valuable source of evaluation, particularly if you experience
a high level of trust and openness in your group.

Ministry Recipients

Whether or not you acknowledge it, persons to whom you minister are evaluating you on a regular basis. It is often said that many
a minister has been "had" for Sunday lunch. Often, you will never
hear your parishioners evaluate you. Sometimes you may learn of
their evaluation of your ministry in hurtful and damaging ways.
There may be individuals who will risk sharing with you their evaluation of your ministry to them. Being human, you may not always
want to hear what they have to say. You may even discount their
positive evaluations of your ministry because they do not "really"
know you.

While most of the evaluation from your parishioners may be tacit, there may be times in the supervisory experience when you will request a more formal evaluation from them. Ministry recipients may be asked to help you be accountable for measuring the progress you make on your learning goals. The people for whom you are providing ministry can be a valuable source of feedback. You will need courage and determination to seek out this evaluation and then to pay attention to it.

Modes and Manners of Evaluation

Evaluation should occur at every step of the supervisory experience. In the early stages of supervision, evaluation will be necessary in order to ascertain which areas need to be focused upon in the **learning covenant.** This will involve self-evaluation by the student and discussion with other members of the supervisory team.

In the middle stages of supervision, evaluation will occur on both a formal and informal level. In formal ways the field supervisor and/ or lay committee will be meeting with you on a regular basis, sharing feedback and evaluation concerning your ministry in the **placement** and your progress toward attaining the learning goals and objectives. Evaluation of progress on the learning goals at this point in the semester may prompt a revision of the learning covenant.

Your school may require that you and your supervisor(s) complete periodic reports to keep the field education director apprised of your learning experience. You may note areas of discussion in supervisory meetings, progress on the learning goals, and areas for future discussion and growth. A routine part of the **supervisory conference** between you and your **field supervisor** and/or **lay committee** will be a verbal evaluation of these things, in addition to that which is noted in writing.

At the end of the supervisory experience there will be a formal written evaluation. This, too, will vary from school to school. If appropriate feedback of your work has been shared throughout the supervisory experience, none of the information on this final evaluation should be of any surprise to you. It only summarizes the issues dealt with during the supervisory experience. Many schools include a place on this form for the field supervisor and/or lay committee to recommend a grade for the learning acquired in the supervisory experience.

Other means of evaluation include the writing of ministry reports, such as **verbatim reports,** case studies, or ministry events. These reports will often be the basis for evaluation of your reaction/actions to real ministry events. They should also help shape your understanding of the ways in which you relate to people and circumstances. These ministry reports are designed to help you affirm ministry skills you already possess and acknowledge areas which need further growth and development.

Feedback needs to be an ongoing part of the supervisory process. This will afford you the opportunity for making intelligent and informed adjustments in your ministry while there is still time to practice the new behaviors and evaluate the effectiveness of the changes made. The ever-present process of feedback and evaluation will help reduce your anxiety about the quality of your ministry experience. Also, dealing with smaller issues when they occur can help you deal with the issues more appropriately if they arise again. This also inhibits the buildup of hostilities or frustrations over issues ignored and left to grow and fester.

Issues in Evaluation

Unfortunately there is no set list of expectations for ministers. Ministry needs vary according to the various settings in which ministry can be performed. Some ministry skills and competencies are fairly universal in their appropriateness to all forms of ministry. Your school may have developed a list of competencies considered as minimal requirements for a student to hold in order to be ready for ministry. Here is a list of some of the issues that you and your supervisor might consider when evaluating your ability to minister.[1]

---

1. This list is only a start. It is by no means an exhaustive list of qualities, characteristics, attitudes, and skills for effective ministry. In addition to my research with church music field supervisors and the competency listings and evaluation forms of colleagues from other seminaries, I have received help from the following books:

Dorothy L. Williams, Milo L. Brekke, and Daniel O. Aleshire, *Profiles in Ministry: Interpretive Manual for Stage I* (Vandalia, Ohio: Association of Theological Schools in the United States and Canada, 1986).

Doran McCarty, *Supervising Ministry Students* (Atlanta: Home Mission Board, 1986), 87–94.

1. *Personal integrity:* Are you a person of your word? Do you live a principle-centered life or do your principles shift according to the current situation?

2. *Personal faith commitment:* Do you have an active and dynamic faith? Is your faith real? Are you able to share your faith in appropriate ways?

3. *Personal spiritual discipline:* Do you have an active devotional life, including the use of the Scriptures, prayer, and meditation?

4. *Trustworthiness:* Can you be trusted to carry out responsibilities without constant supervision? Are you dependable in completing tasks and assignments? Do you keep confidences?

5. *Honesty and openness in relationships:* Do you relate to others in genuine ways? Are you able to reveal yourself to others in appropriate ways? Do you value the worth of other people?

6. *Flexibility:* Are you flexible in dealing with your own life and the lives of others around you? Are you flexible to the point of having no firm convictions? Are you rigid and unbending? Can you be spontaneous?

7. *Ability to relate with warmth and interest:* Do you communicate to others that you are interested in them as persons and not just as objects of your ministry?

8. *Sensitivity to the gifts of others:* Do you need to be the center of attention or can you truly find joy in the gifts of other people? Does your sensitivity to the gifts and abilities of others mean that you find little worth in your own gifts and abilities?

9. *Self-discipline:* Are you a disciplined person in the good sense of the word? Are you punctual in completing your tasks? Do you value the time of other people? Are you able to provide personal initiative for your ministry or must you be prodded and reminded by others? Are you able to exer-

cise appropriate control of yourself—your emotions, your use of time, money management, etc.?

10. *Criticism:* Are you able to give constructive feedback to others? How do you respond to constructive criticism? How do you respond when others criticize you harshly?

11. *Listening:* Do you listen to others with your ears, your eyes, and your heart? Do you talk too much or do you spend your listening time shaping your own responses while others are talking to you?

12. *Decision-making skills:* Can you make decisions easily? Do you rely on other people to make decisions so that you will not have to take responsibility for the outcomes of those decisions? Are you too quick to make decisions without considering all of the consequences of your decisions?

13. *Stress:* How do you react to stress in your life? Do you work well under pressure? If so, what effect does this have on your other relationships? How does the presence of stress manifest itself in your life—irritability, overeating, procrastination, task-oriented approach to work, etc.?

14. *Conflict:* Can you identify various forms of conflict? Do you know different ways of confronting or dealing with conflict? What is your personal style of conflict management? Do you enjoy conflict? Do you avoid conflict?

15. *Anger:* How do you handle the anger of others? Do you recognize the presence of anger in your own life? What kinds of people or situations cause you to become angry? How do you deal with your anger?

16. *Self-awareness:* How open are you with yourself about your strengths and weaknesses, your likes and dislikes, the way your past has influenced the way you behave in the present?

17. *Self-concept:* How do you view and value yourself? Are you able to receive the affirmation of others without discounting their compliments, or are you always seeking praise

from others? Are you able to appropriately affirm yourself and your gifts, skills, and abilities?

18. *Encouragement:* Are you able to offer words of encouragement to others in appropriate ways? Are you too critical? Do you offer empty words of praise?

19. *Collegiality:* Do you work well with others? Do you always need to be in control? Do you share in group processes or do you tend to be passive in group situations?

20. *Sensitivity to diversity:* Are you open to the diversity among other peoples and beliefs? Are you aware of areas where you need to broaden your understanding of cultures and perspectives different from your own?

21. *Personal care:* Do you take good care of yourself—emotionally, physically, and spiritually? Do you have an appropriate sense of self-esteem? Are you well-groomed and neatly dressed?

22. *Sense of humor:* Are you able to use humor effectively in relating to others? Do you laugh *with* others or *at* others? Are you able to laugh at yourself?

23. *Authority:* Do you have a healthy sense of personal authority? How do you react to those in authority over you? Does the gender, age, race, or socio-economic background of the person in authority over you affect the way you respond?

24. *Sexuality:* Are you comfortable with your own sexuality? How well do you relate with persons of the opposite sex? How do relate with persons of the same sex?

25. *Leadership skills:* Do you have an understanding of the various styles of leadership? Do you provide leadership that is manipulative, controlling, passive, aggressive, etc.? Are you able to enlist and motivate others to assist you in ministry?

26. *Organizational skills:* Are you able to plan your ministry and implement your plans easily? Are you able to prioritize your work, giving appropriate attention to important matters and not getting caught up in minutia? Are you able to

delegate tasks to others, equipping them to do the necessary work, trusting them to do what you asked, and accepting their work even if it is accomplished in a different manner than you would have?

27. *Caring skills:* Are you able to provide care for others in a variety of contexts—crisis intervention, hospital visitation, grief ministry, marriage counseling, social ministry, pastoral care, and counseling?

28. *Worship leadership skills:* Can you plan and lead meaningful worship experiences?

29. *Teaching skills:* Are you able to teach others utilizing a variety of teaching methodologies based on the various learning styles?

30. *Integration of theory and practice:* Are you able to put together the things you have learned in the classroom and through reading with the practice of ministry with real people?

31. *Communication skills:* Are you able to communicate effectively with others through verbal and written means? Are you able to articulate ideas on a variety of levels so that people of differing ages and backgrounds might understand you on their own levels?

32. *Understanding of structures:* Do you understand the formal and informal power structures at work in your place of ministry? Are you able to work within these structures?

This list could go on. You will want to add skills specifically related to your vocational calling. This limited list is included here to help you identify some of the ministry competencies that you may be evaluated on in the course of your supervised ministry experiences.

Do not let this list overwhelm you! No one is competent in all of these areas. Now, while you have the opportunity for supervision by a caring, more experienced minister, you can work toward improving your competence in these and other important areas as you seek to grow into the person and minister God has called you to be.

Glossary

William T. Pyle and Mary Alice Seals

Action Plan: A plan for the process of integrating self-understanding, cognitive data, and practical skills in the practice of ministry.

Assessment Instruments: Personality preference and temperament indicators used to increase self-awareness and self-understanding.

Association for Theological Field Education (ATFE): An organization of theological field educators from member seminaries of the Association of Theological Schools (ATS). The purpose of ATFE is "to provide a forum for the identification, study, and action on issues of significance to theological field education; to develop resources and services pertinent to the task of theological field education; and to cooperate with other groups in advancing the task of theological field education" (from By-Laws of the Association of Theological Field Education).

Block Placement: A full-time ministry placement in which the student does not take additional academic courses.

Call Statement: A component of the vocational management planning pool. It focuses on why you are in ministry, how you are gifted for ministry, and the ministry role toward which you see yourself moving.

Case Study Method: An approach to learning, which uses the analysis of actual events so that students develop analytical skills, decision-making skills, and learn to apply theory to concrete situations.

Case: A written description of an actual event in ministry in which a decision must be made.

Clinical Pastoral Education (CPE): A structured learning experience which focuses on the student's ministry with people. Students learn from that ministry through reflection, dialogue, and evaluation with other students and supervisors.

Concurrent Placement: A ministry placement in which the student takes academic courses in addition to field education.

Critical Reflection: The process of examining your actions in order to identify and clarify your assumptions.

Data-Gathering: A means for bringing samples of your ministry to supervision for examination and reflection. Examples of data gathering methods include case studies, verbatim reports, and process notes.

Dreams-Needs-Wants Statement: A component of a vocational management pool. It focuses on your dreams, needs, and wants, taking seriously your natural desires and wishes.

Field Service: A ministry training program which focuses on providing ministry to the community.

Field Supervisor: An experienced minister who, through regular meetings with the student minister, assists the student in developing the learning covenant, reflecting on ministry events, and evaluating the ministry experience.

Field Work: A ministry training program in which students gain ministry experience while earning additional income.

Incident Report: A form of data-gathering which focuses on your emotional response and/or ministry performance in a ministry event.

Journal: A form of data-gathering that allows you to reflect on a number of issues you might encounter in your supervised ministry experience. A journal is an ongoing written reflection recorded over an extended period of time.

Lay Committee: A group of five to seven persons who have agreed to serve as a part of your supervisory team.

Learning Covenant: A document developed to provide direction for your learning during a specific period of time. It normally consists of three components: goals, action plans, and means of evaluation. It is mutually developed by the student and field supervisor.

Learning/Serving Agreement: An agreement between the student, supervisor, and/or placement institution. It focuses on the work or ministry you will be providing. It contains information commonly contained in job descriptions. In some schools the learning/serving agreement may be referred to as a supervisory agreement or placement contract.

Ministry Event: An event in ministry which is the basis for written or oral reports in the supervisory experience. These reports help students gain insight into the ways in which they practice ministry, their assumptions about ministry, and evaluation of their ministry skills.

Mission Statement: A component of a vocational management planning pool. It is a concise statement of your purpose in life. It becomes a basis for decision-making.

Peer Reflection Group: A small group of student ministers who meet regularly to provide support, nurture, and supervision to each other. Normally students bring written accounts of ministry experiences for analysis and feedback.

Placement: The arena in which students are engaged in supervised ministry experiences (such as churches, hospitals, social agencies). Placements best-suited for supervised ministry experiences are those in which students are given significant opportunities for doing ministry while engaged in supervision with a qualified field supervisor.

Process Notes: A form of data-gathering which focuses on a specific ministry issue over a period of time.

Strengths Inventory: A self-assessment process that provides insights into your gifts, abilities, and potential strengths.

Supervision: A process of integrating self-understanding, cognitive data, and practical skills in the practice of ministry.

Supervisory Conference: A weekly meeting of the student and field supervisor. Its goal is to develop the student as a person and minister. The primary means of accomplishing this goal includes self-directed learning (learning covenant) and reflection on ministry events.

Theological Field Education: The intentional use of ministry experience as a learning opportunity. This approach combines experience, service, and employment, with the primary emphasis on the student's development as a person and minister.

Theological Reflection: The process of examining the events of life through the lens of faith in order to integrate experience and faith.

Values Statement: A component of a vocational management planning pool. It is a listing of those values most important to you.

Verbatim Report: A form of data-gathering which focuses on the communication that occurred during a ministry event. Normally a verbatim report includes a transcript of the communication that occurred as remembered by the writer.

Vision Statement: A component of a vocational management planning pool. It is a clear statement of your strategic plan for your future.

Vocational Management Plan: A process for developing immediate short-term and long-term goals. It consists of two major structures: a planning pool and a goals section.

Vocational Management Planning Pool: The first structure in a vocational management plan. It consists of five components: a call statement, a values statement, a mission statement, a vision statement, and a dreams-needs-wants statement. These five statements provide the basis for developing vocational management goals.

Appendix 1

Assessment Instrument Descriptions

Ronald Hornecker and Gary Pearson

California Psychological Inventory uses twenty scales to identify preferences in four areas: interpersonal style, adjustment, achievement needs, and cognitive style. It has implications for managerial potential work orientation, leadership potential, social maturity, and creative potential.

Disc is an instrument that is helpful in understanding differences in personality types and responses. It is also useful in indicating one's own type and how he/she will tend to interact with others.

Firo-B (Fundamental Interpersonal Relationship Orientation-B) reflects how an individual establishes and maintains social and affectional relationships with others and the extent to which he or she seeks to establish control by making decisions and assuming responsibility. It also provides an indication of the degree of initiative the person takes in these three areas or leaves that initiative in the hands of others.

Myers-Briggs Type Indicator reflects preferences in four areas: where one prefers to focus attention, how one acquires information, how one makes decisions, and how one is oriented toward the outer world. It is valuable for understanding one's self as well as other persons and relationships.

Profiles of Ministry provides an estimate of how likely an individual is to express various personal characteristics (both positive and negative) in ministry as well as undertaking various approaches in the pactice of ministry. It makes use of a case study booklet and an oral interview.

16 PF reflects a person's preference and strength on sixteen bipolar personality factors. Unlike many other personality tests, it detects and describes normal personality. With computer scoring it indicates some basic personality characteristics as well as some comparisons with various occupational groupings.

Taylor-Johnson Temperament Analysis reflects nine bipolar personality traits that are significant in personal adjustment and in interpersonal relationships. It can be used in a criss-cross manner, taken by one person on another. It can also be used in the early identification of emotionally troubled persons.

Tennessee Self-concept is an instrument to indicate how an individual perceives his/her physical, moral-ethical, personal, family, and social self. It also indicates one's self-criticism, self-identity, self-satisfaction, and acceptance.

Theological School Inventory provides a description of an individual's motivations, interests, self-reported skills, and biographical characteristics as related to ministry. Information from the inventory is intended to be used by the student to explore personal and career concerns in relation to ministy.

Appendix 2

A Model Verbatim Report[1]

Walter Jackson

Confidential Ministry Report

A Verbatim Record of Ministry to Mr. J. Doe

Jack Smith, pastor, Second Church, September 29, 1983

Introduction

John Doe is a forty-nine-year-old businessman, has a good marriage to Jane, their children—Billy, seventeen, and Jessica, thirteen—both live at home. All are baptized members of Second Church, all are faithful in attendance, support, and leadership.

John's Sunday School teacher reported to me that John was unusually quiet in class that morning, but three times the teacher noticed John crying quietly. The lesson had dealt with the raising of Lazarus. John did not attend morning worship today after the class meeting.

John's father died about sixteen months ago. Although they had been exceptionally close, John had been unable to express grief about his father publicly. Jane had spoken to me with concern about this three months ago.

I had made several visits to John. Although we talked about his father on two occasions, John always spoke with bright, happy tones.

---

1. Walter C. Jackson, *School of Theology Supervised Ministry Experience Manual: Instructions, Contracts and Report Forms* (Department of Ministry, The Southern Baptist Theological Seminary, 1994), 21–25.

I have been pastor here a little over two years.

I was anxious about the visit. I was hoping John was dealing with his grief but I was afraid something else had caused his apparent distress today. My hope was to help him with his grief, but I was open to anything.

I called and asked John if I could visit. He seemed eager, and invited me to come over. I found him alone at home. He turned off the football game and began to talk rapidly. Tears filled his eyes as he spoke. He sat tensely on the edge of his easy chair. I sat on the sofa, close enough to touch him, but sitting back . . .

Interpersonal Exchange

J1 Jane and the kids are at the youth choir festival over in Central City . . . (eyes very red).

P1 Oh, I forget about . . .

J2 (Interrupts as if he did not hear me.) I insisted that they go without me (blows nose); I'd be no good to anyone over there, or here for that matter . . .

P2 (I interrupted too.) I don't understand, John.

J3 I just can't stop this stupid weeping; it's as if my tear ducts have become water fountains with bad leaks (wipes eyes).

P3 What . . . (too late, he goes on).

J4 The problem, or really the problems, I have are just too heavy for me, pastor, (gets up and looks out window). I'm just so stirred up, I could chop wood all day, like when I was a kid . . . mom never had to ask me to cut wood as long as I was angry . . . I'd always be way ahead (pause).

P4 What's got you so stirred up like this, John?

J5 It's hard to say, there are so many things (quieter now, sits down again). I can't think straight. (rapidly) The business is going so great; everybody wants to buy insurance in a recession, it's time to move into a larger office, but if I do, I'll wipe out all my profits, and if I do move and sales slump I'll be in a big fix.

P5 (I mumble something, but John goes on.)

J6 Dad always said not to get too much of the cash flow committed to overhead; and (more rapidly) one of my salesmen is drinking too much again; you know Ronald—the class has prayed for him. He's giving me such a bad reputation, but oh, I'd hate to cut him off because of his wife and kids (hangs his head).

P6 What would your father have done if he were still your senior partner, John?

J7 Boy, would I give a lot to talk to him now (tears flow freely now). He always seemed to know what to do—things always turned out so right for him—but he didn't have a drunken employee like Ron.

P7 I wish he were here now for your sake, John.

J8 I cried myself to sleep here in this chair dozens of nights grieving over him so I could hold my head up like a Christian, and I have a lot of peace about him now.

P8 Peace?

J9 He died so quickly I never got to tell him all those things you never think to say until it's too late. (No tears; this sounds solid.) We didn't ever say things like that, but we knew without words (smiles a little) we really were a lot alike, you know (chuckles).

P9 I didn't know him long, John, but I thought you acted more like brothers than father and son.

J10 (Quieter now) I never thought of it that way, but you're right (tears reappear); but that's the end of the line (hangs head, obviously crying again).

P10 I don't understand, John—end of what line?

J11 Oh, it's Billy (looks up, deep feeling in his face). Billy told me he'd never be an insurance agent! Oh, how that hurt! (with much pain)

(Some time here for tears, we talk about Billy's announced plans to start an electronic repair business, about wanting the proceeds of his endowment policy to open a shop instead of going to college—much bitterness—about twenty minutes pass.)

J12 I didn't mean to bend your ear so hard, pastor.

P12 I'm glad you feel free enough to share so much of yourself with me, John.

J13 I've always known you would listen. I should have called you, but I'm glad you called me.

P13 As I see it, John, You've only begun to get things out to look at them. (very anxious) How about us getting together again sometime this week? Thursday?

J14 I'll have to call you. (pause) I really want to, so I'll call after I get to the office tomorrow (seems genuine).

P14 (relieved) I'll make time, John. I wonder if we could share a prayer before I go.

J15 Certainly . . .

Prayer

[Students should write out prayers in full in verbatim reports]

J16 Thank you, pastor, I'll call you first thing tomorrow morning.

P16 I'll be listening for your call, John. Goodbye for now.

Reflections

1. I'm glad I went to see John today.

2. I was very preoccupied with his grief over his father. I was shocked about his deep feelings about his son. I expect his feelings for his father and his son are connected in some way. I'd like some feedback about that.

3. His business difficulties are troublesome, only low priority today. I don't know much about business, but I need to remember to pay attention to him here. Maybe I can help him with his alcoholic employee. The church could help!

4. This man is nearly as old as my own father. I really feel anxious trying to be his minister.

5. I was determined to follow through on this ministry relationship. I also need to find ways to minister to Jane, Billy and maybe even Jessica. I want group help about this.

6. John's grief work with his father's death looks more healthy than I thought.

7. I wonder if an informal place—like lunch—or a formal visit to my office is the best place to see John.

8. I didn't deal directly with theological issues related to John's religious life very much in our conversation. I recognize these three issues:

   - *Hope* as it relates to John's plans for Billy's life; and Billy's hopes.
   - *Idolatry* in terms the grandfather-father-son life continuity.
   - Potential processes of *alienation* that might reach dynamic proportions between John and Billy; the potential for reconciliation between them, etc.

Evaluation

1. At least one Sunday School teacher believes me when I say I care about the church members. My asking them to tell me about needs paid off in this instance.

2. I was very anxious, but I showed good pastoral initiative by going to see John; took initiative also at P6 and P13.

3. I was preoccupied with John's delayed grief over his father's death; was glad I pushed that issue. It led to the most pressing problem, his relationship to Billy.

4. I took the lead at P6 and P7, then followed him at P8 and P10. The conversation seemed to be balanced.

5. I couldn't remember how things happened between J11 and J12.

6. I was consciously expressing gratitude as a pastoral blessing at P12. I think that was well timed.

7. My attempt to continue the relationship seemed successful, though I felt clumsy.

8. I didn't follow up on how Jane was doing, or the children.

9. I missed an opportunity to plan responses to John's need.

10. I think my preoccupation with John's delayed grief blinded me to many other things I could have done.